Mandala

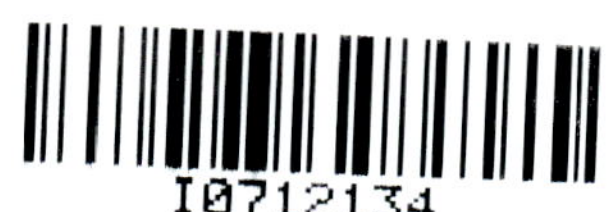

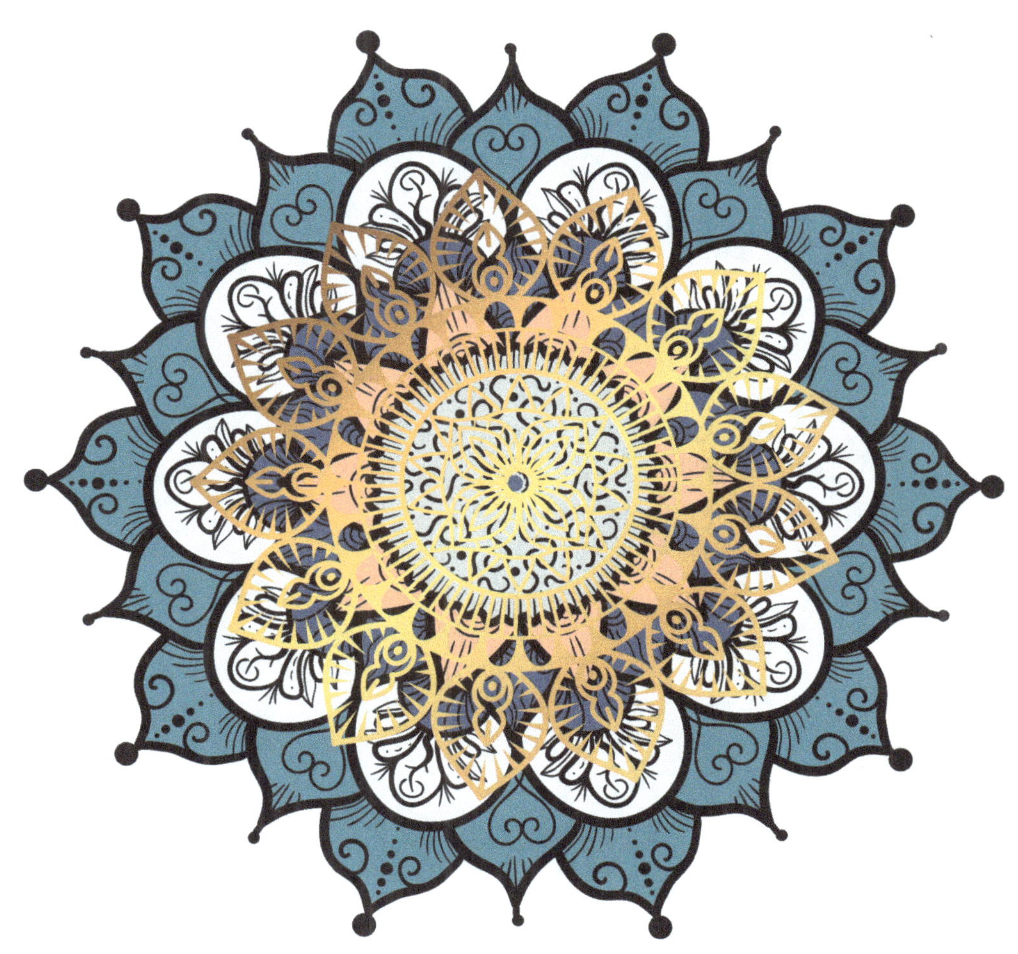

Art Workbook 2

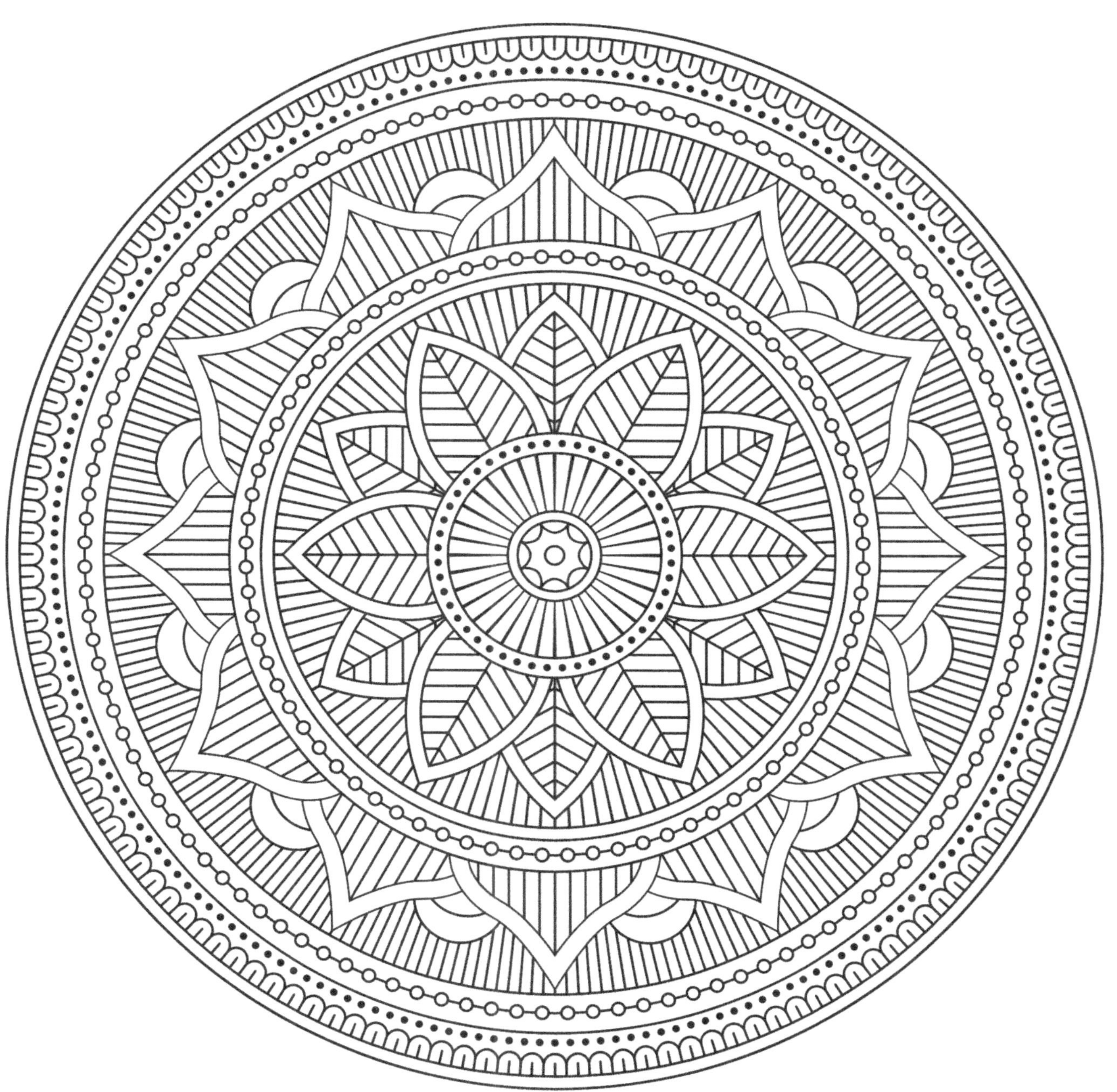

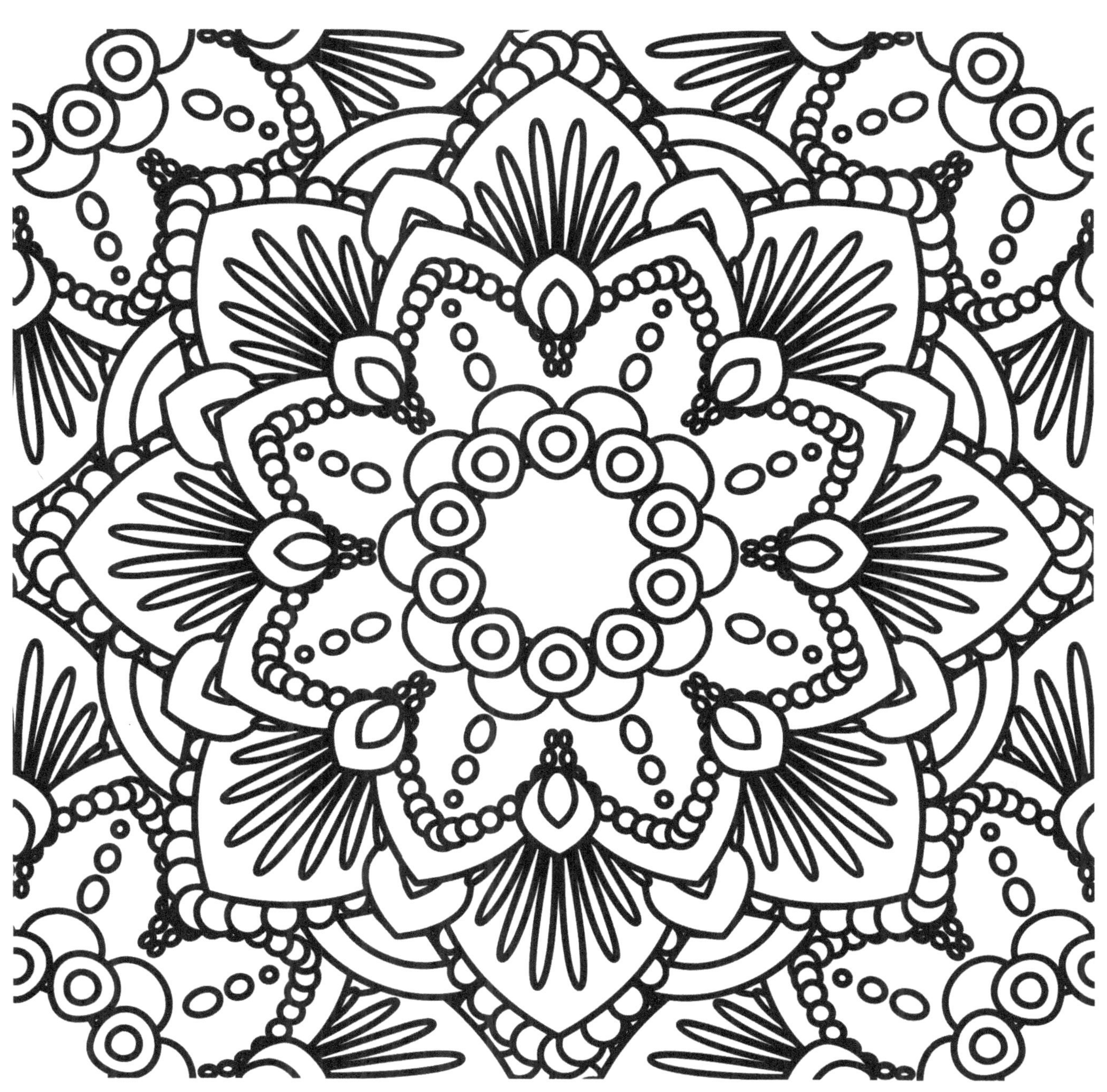

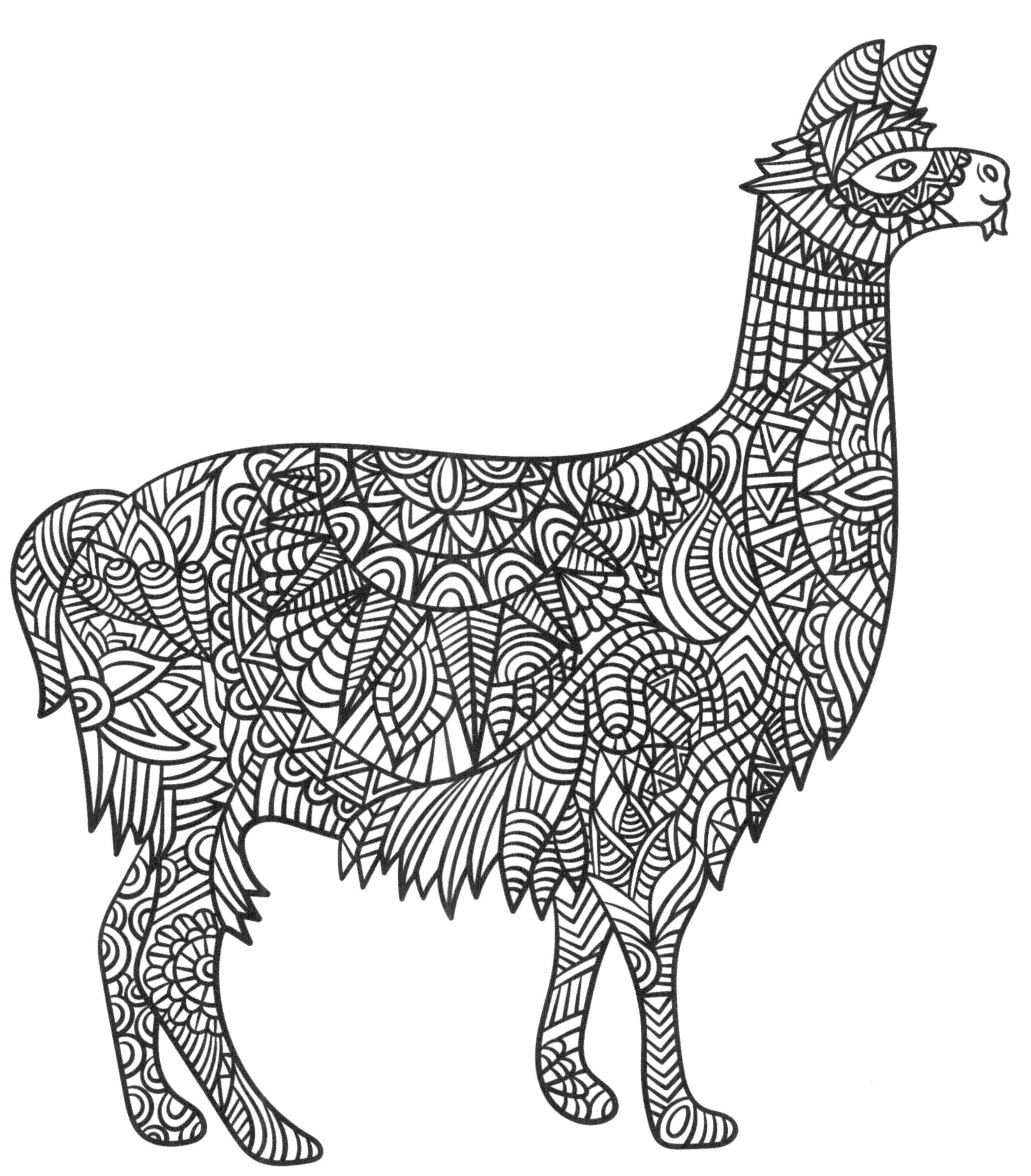

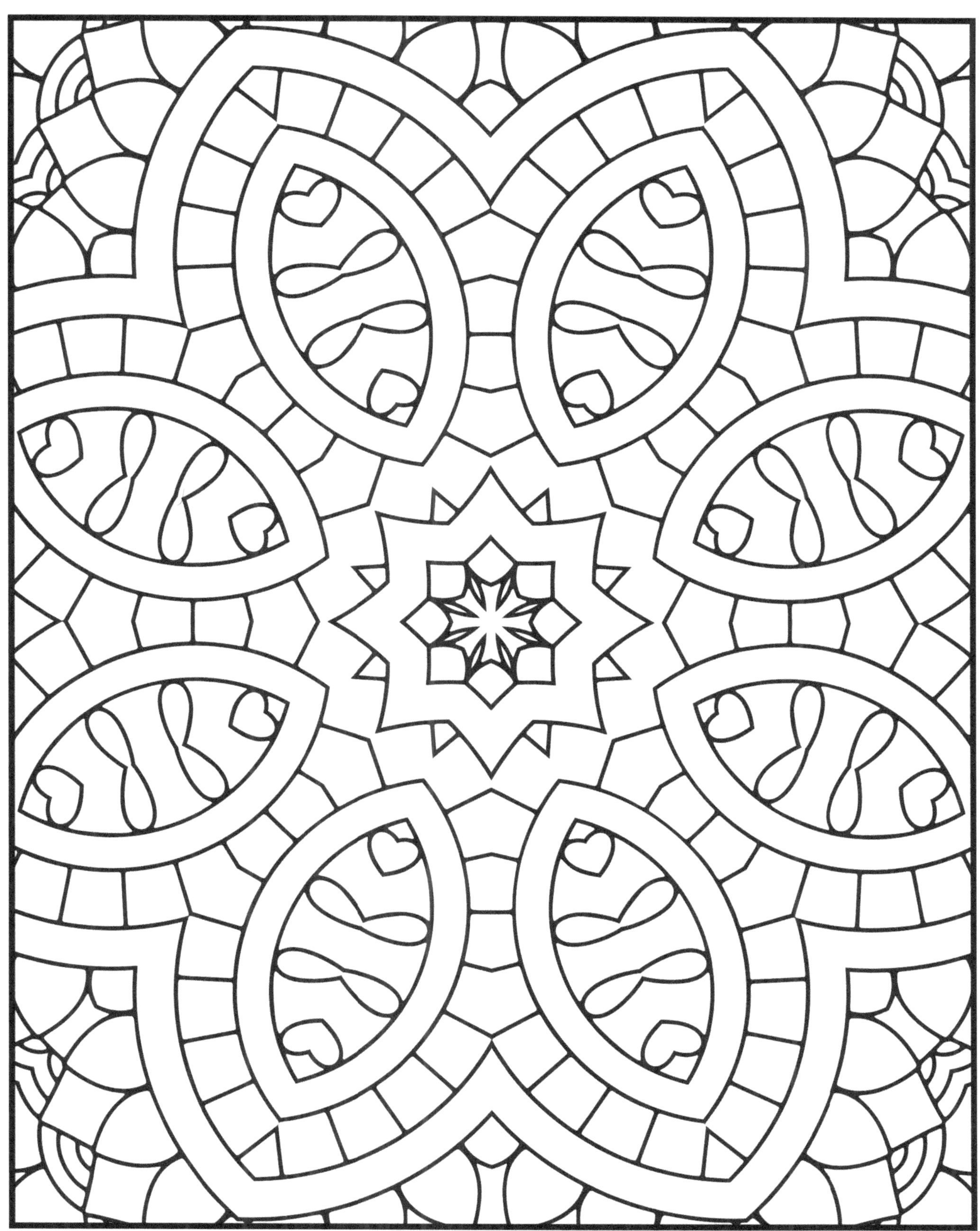

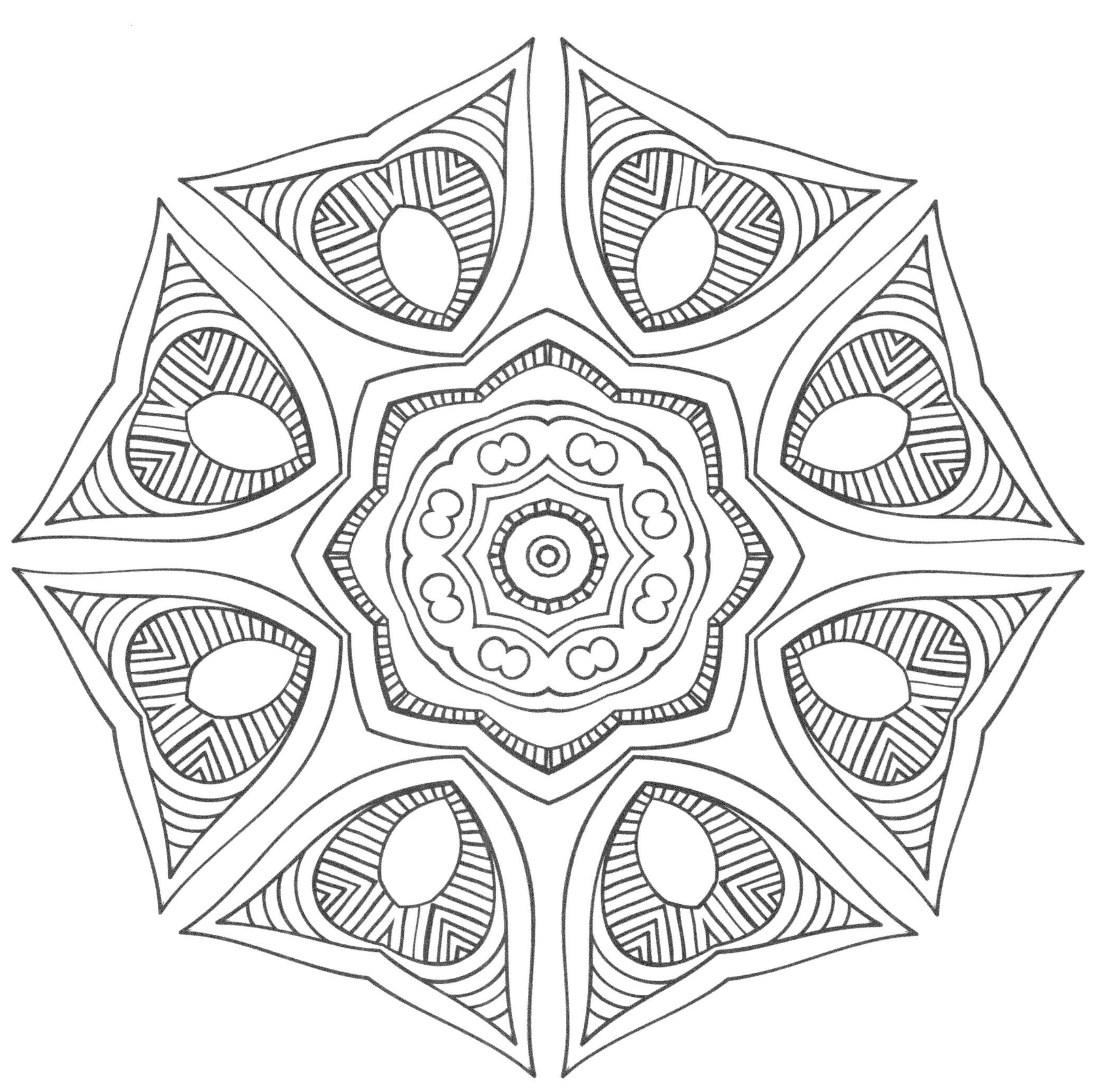

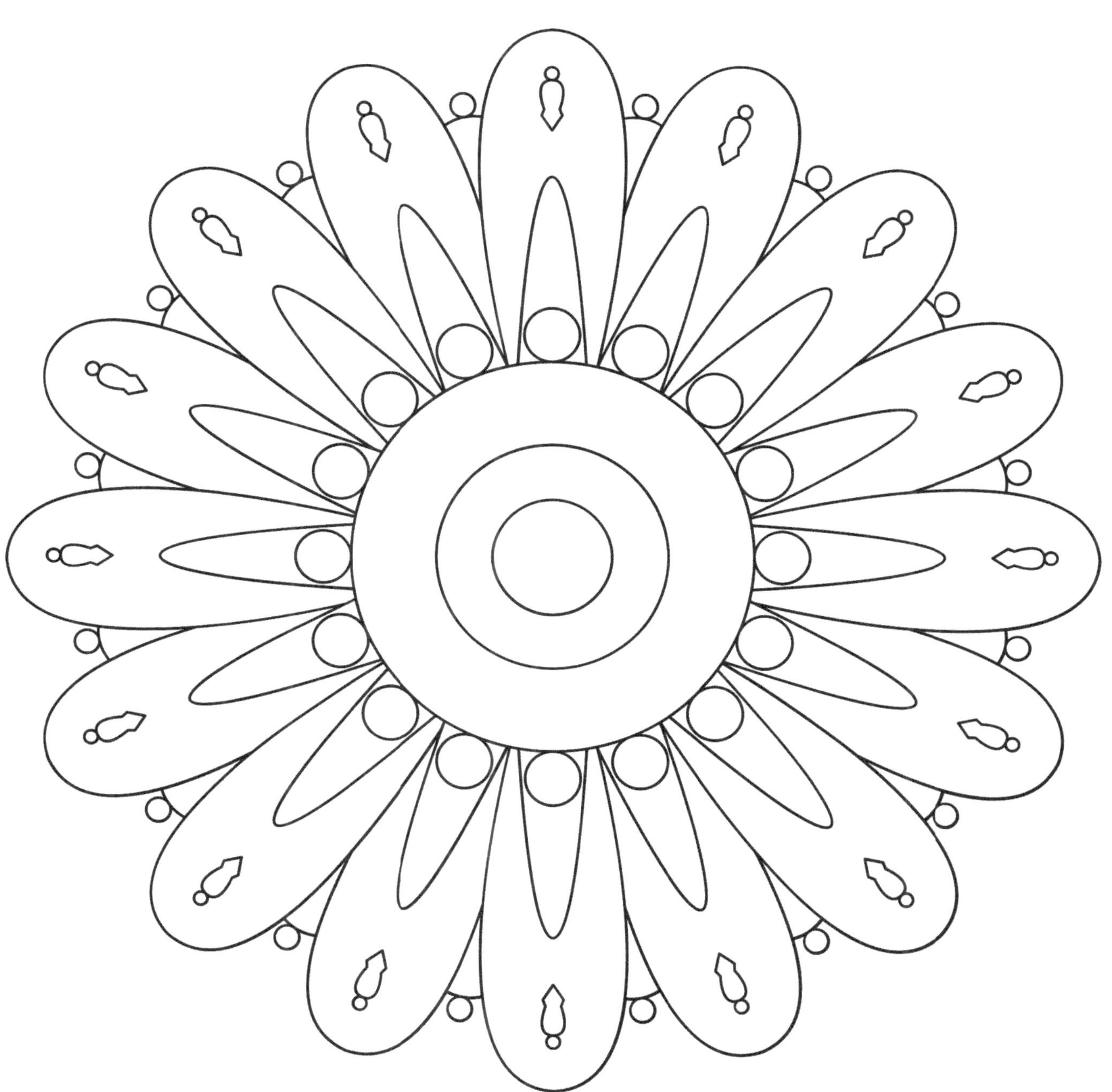

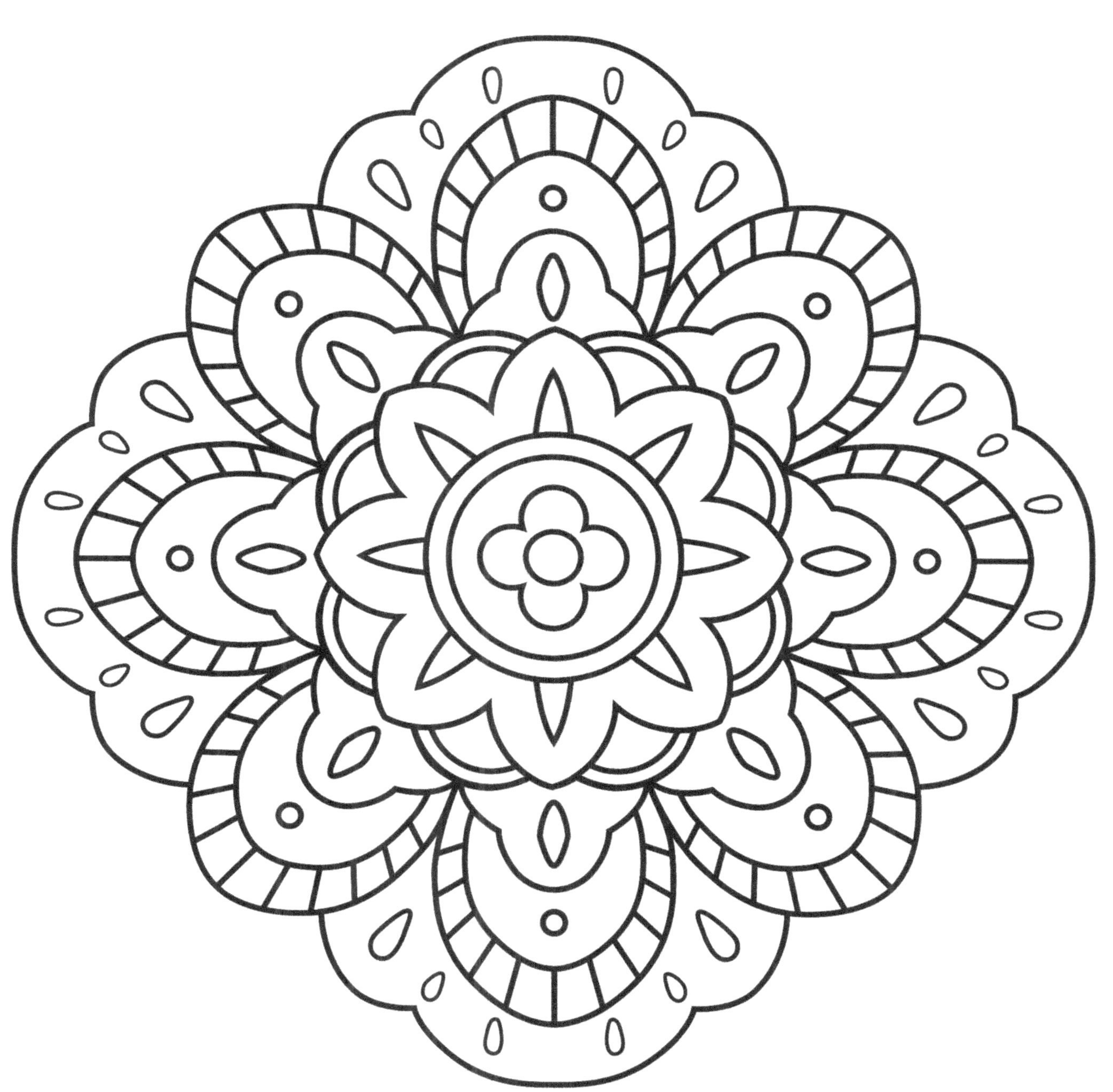

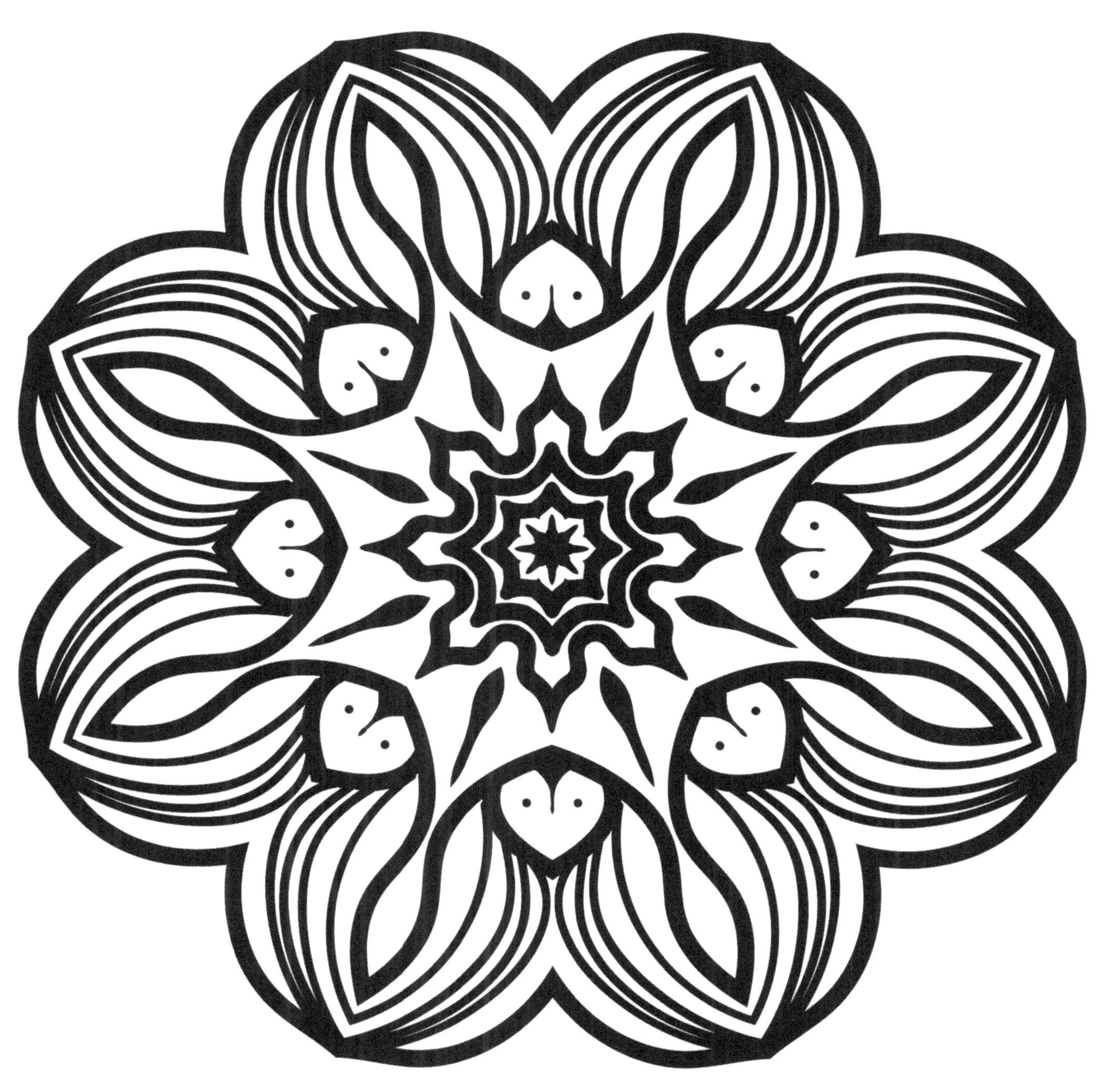

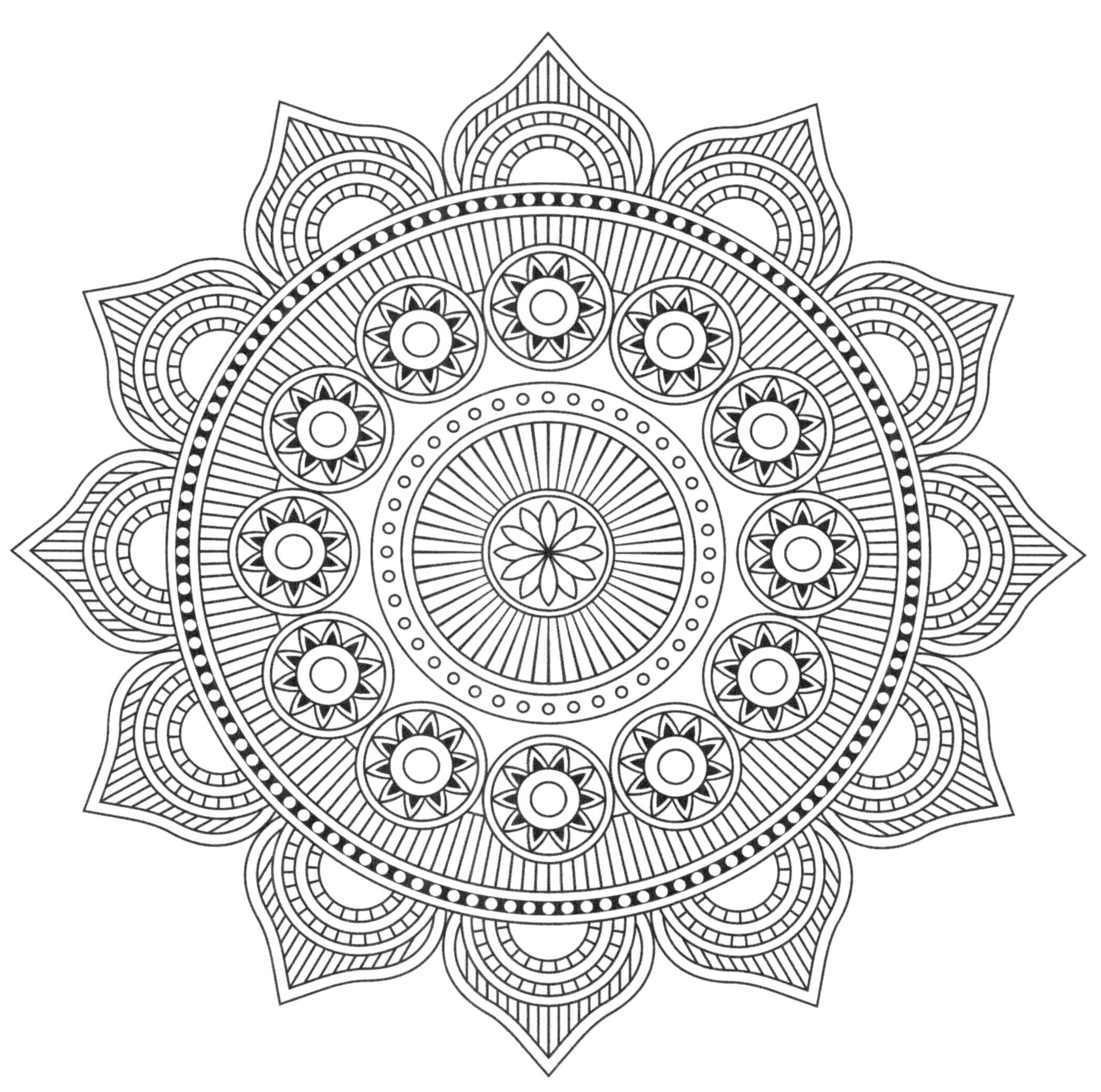

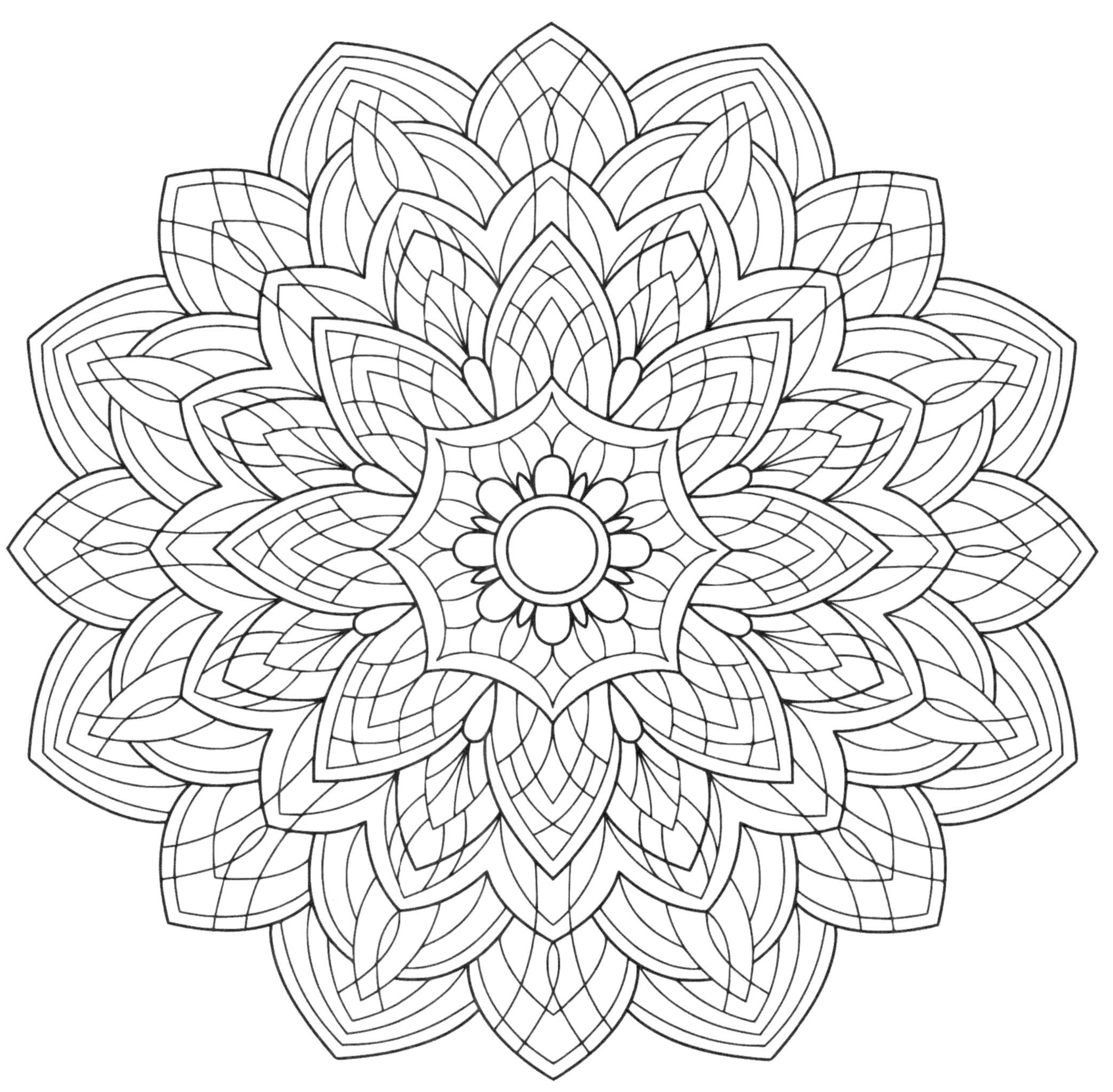

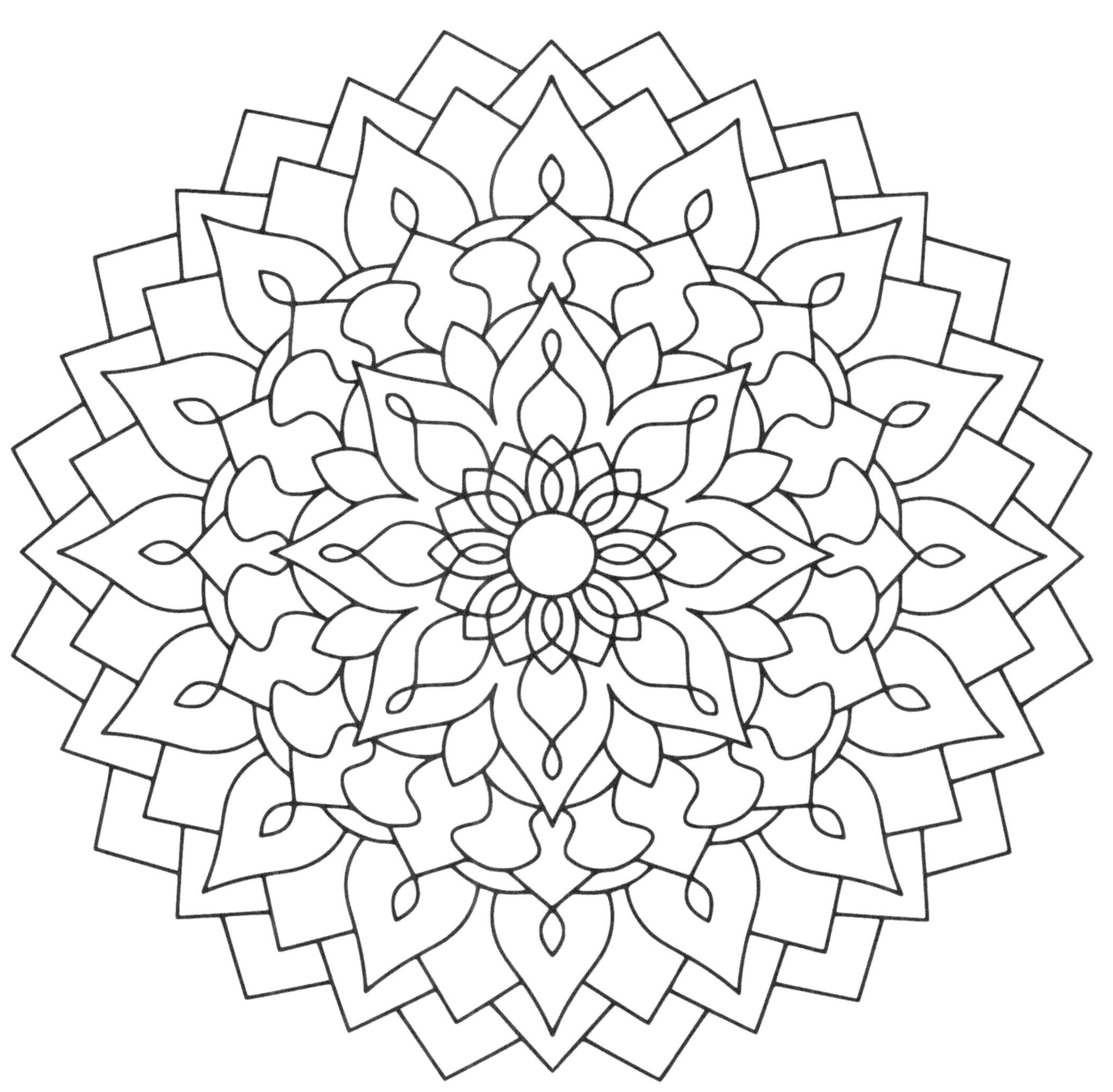

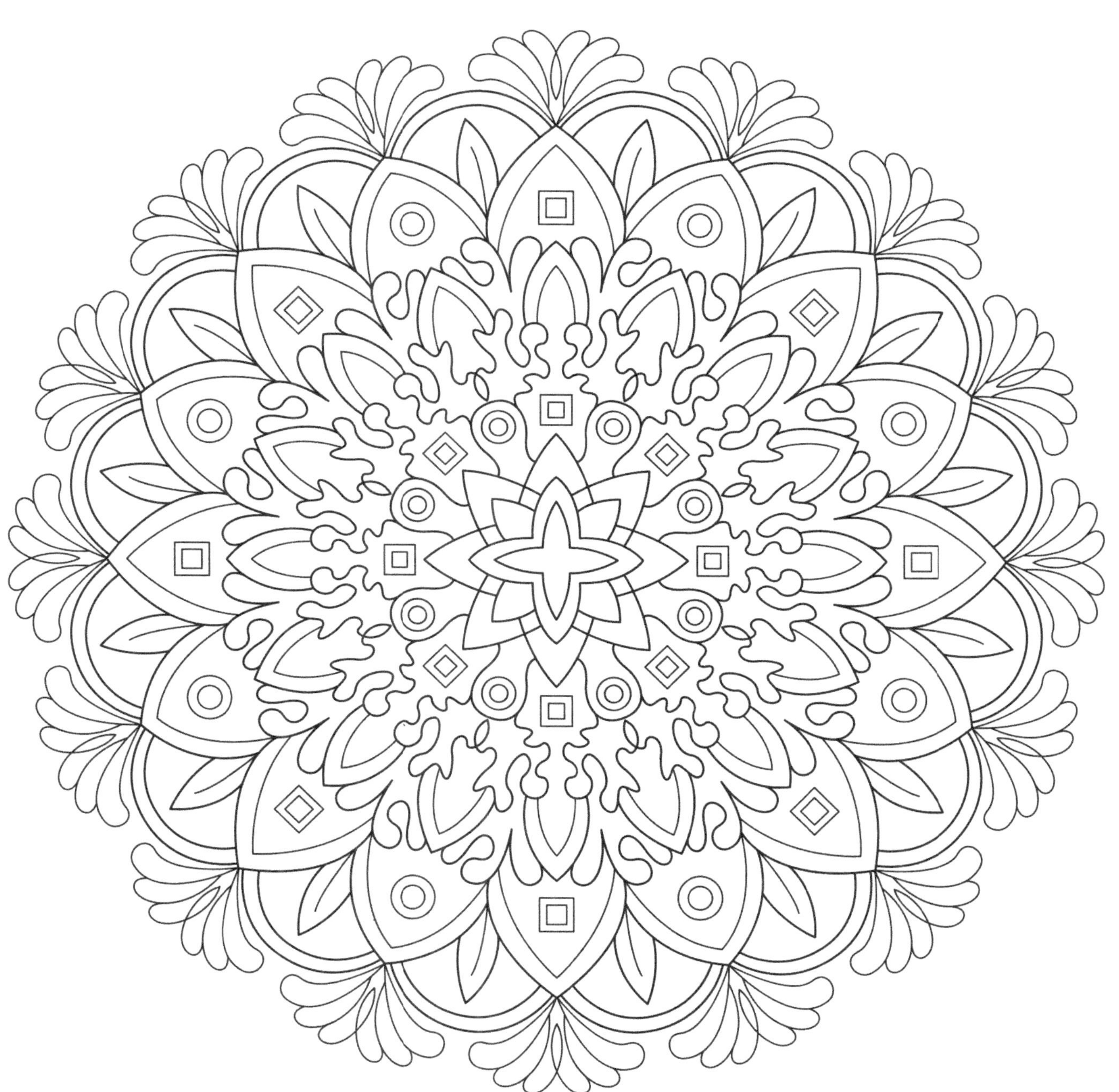

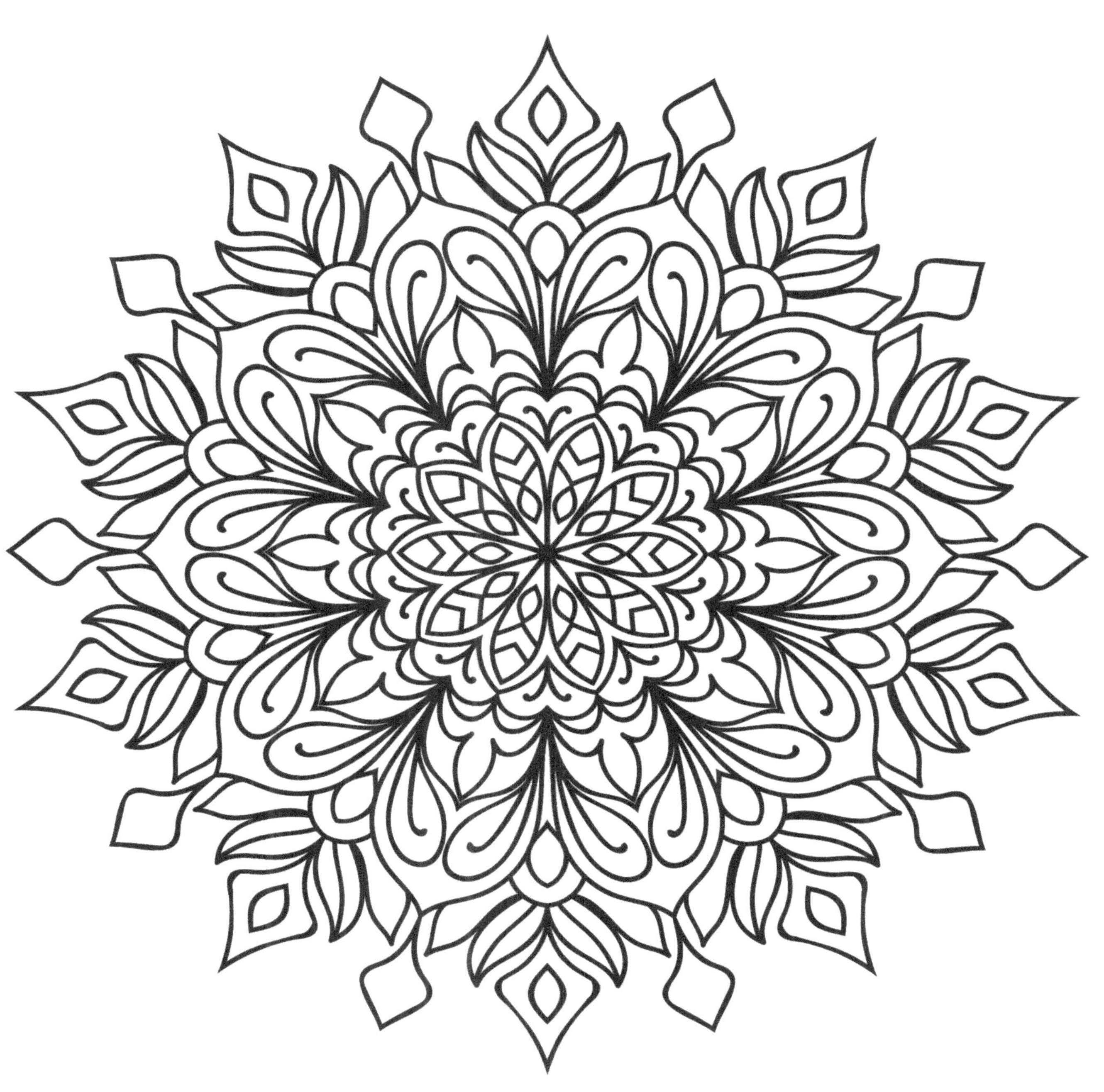

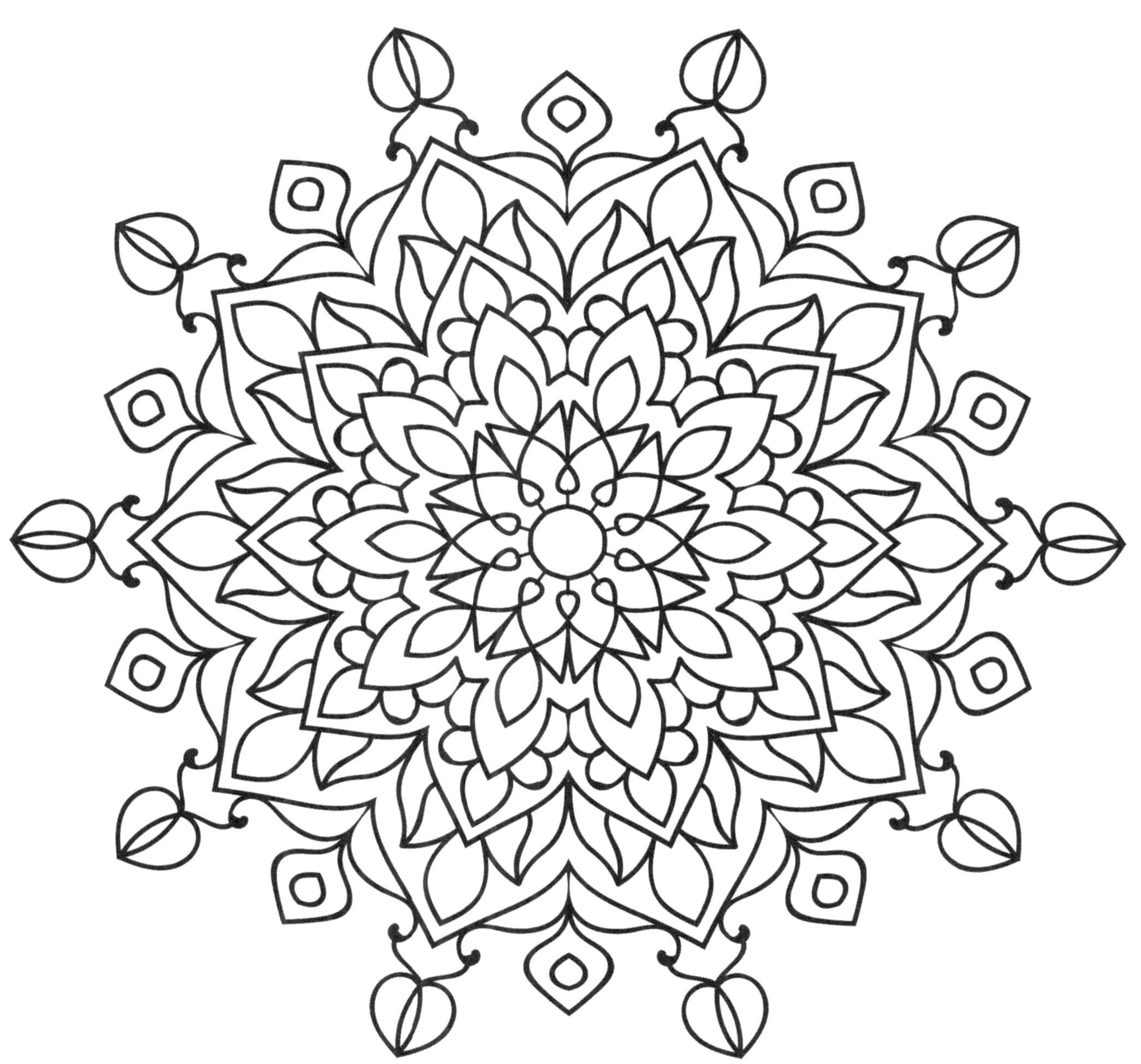

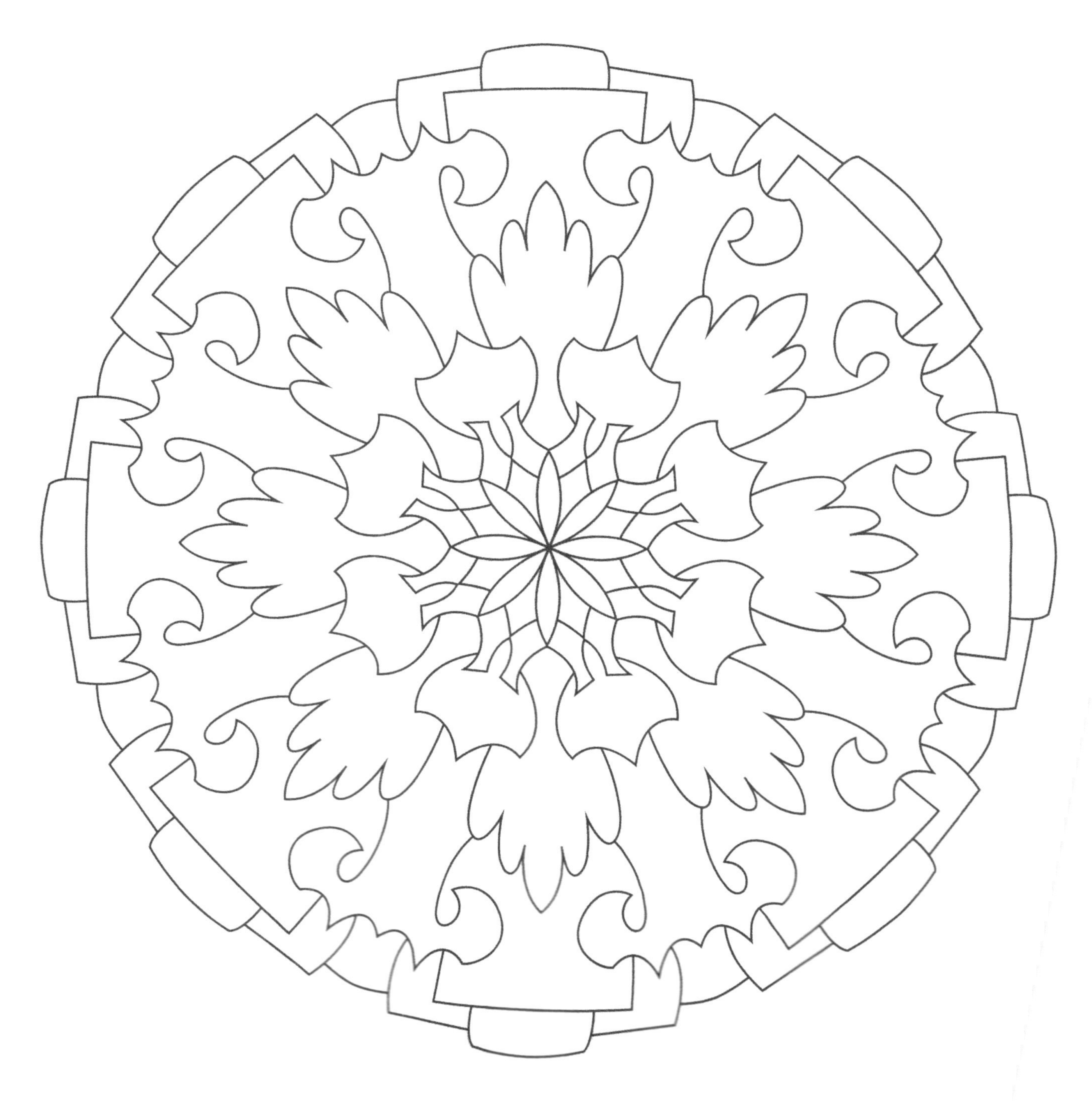

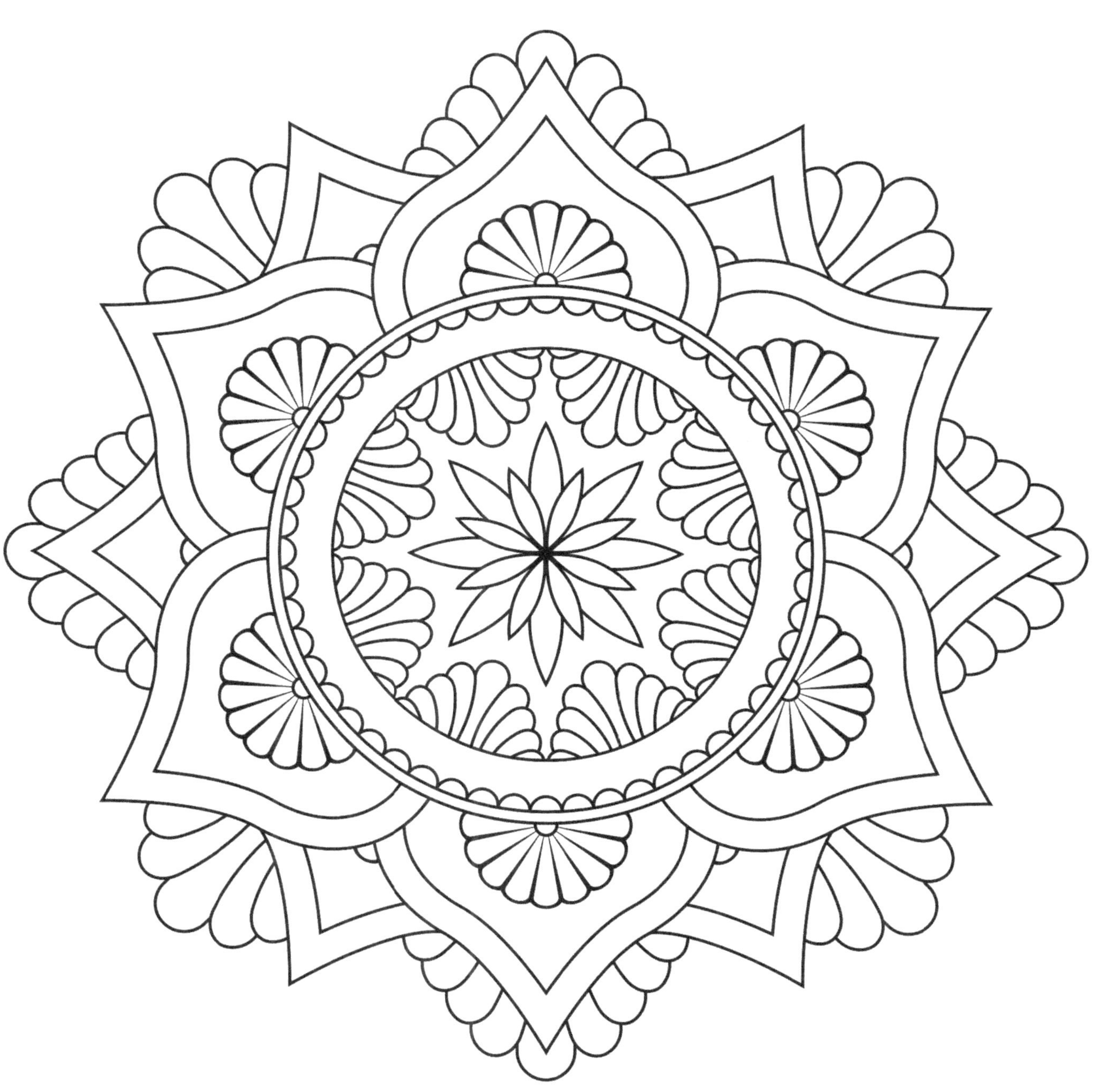

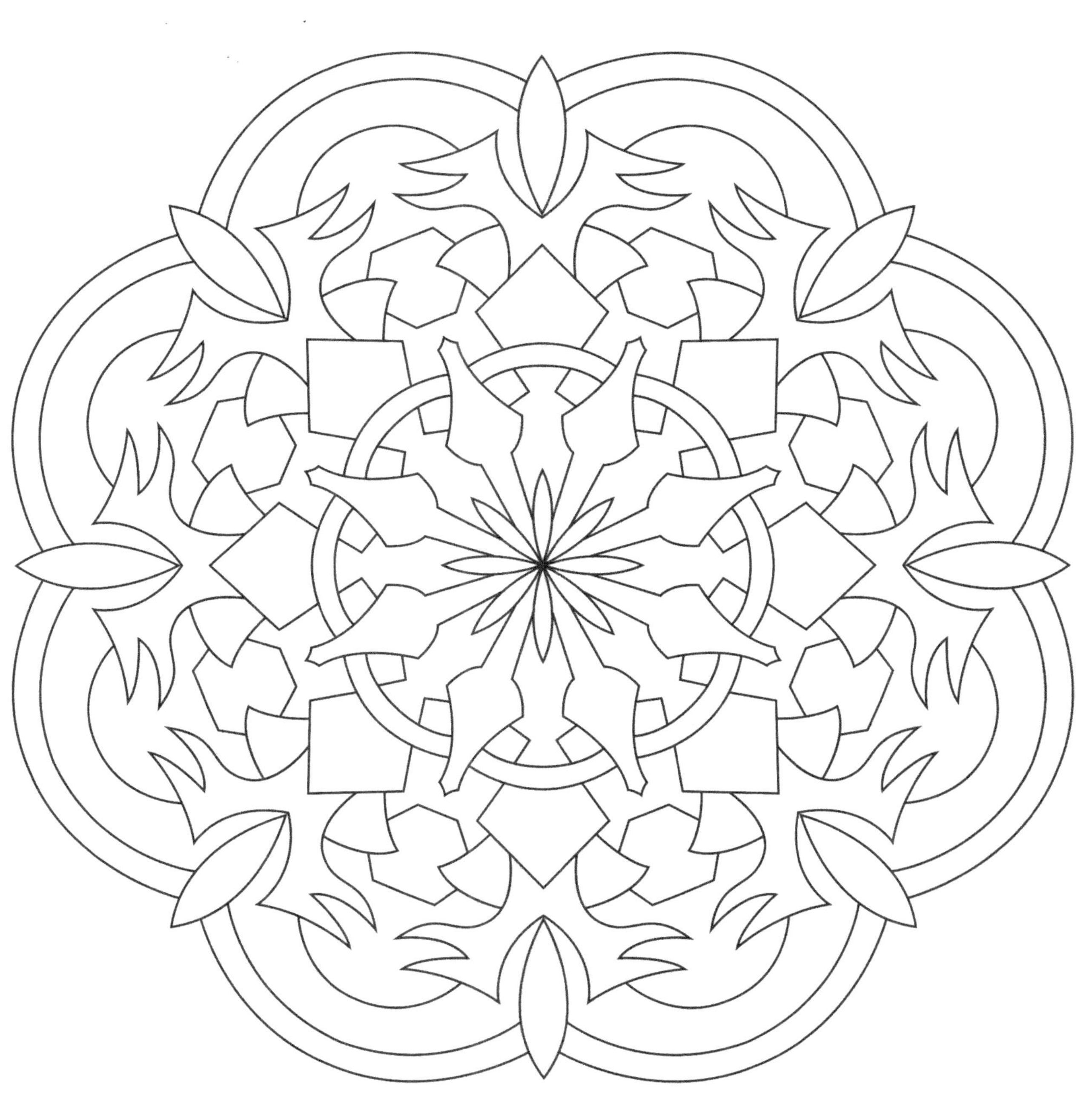

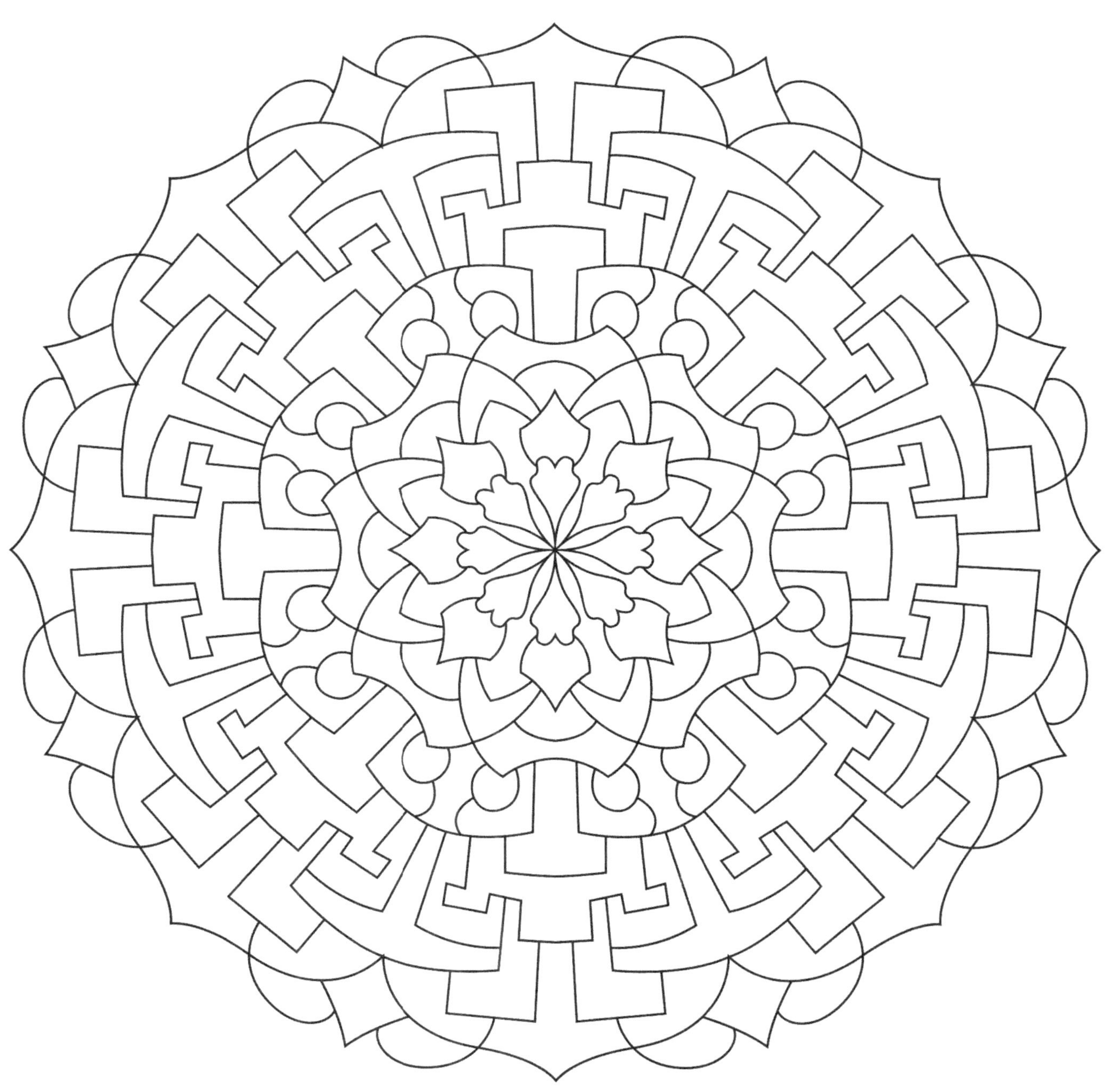

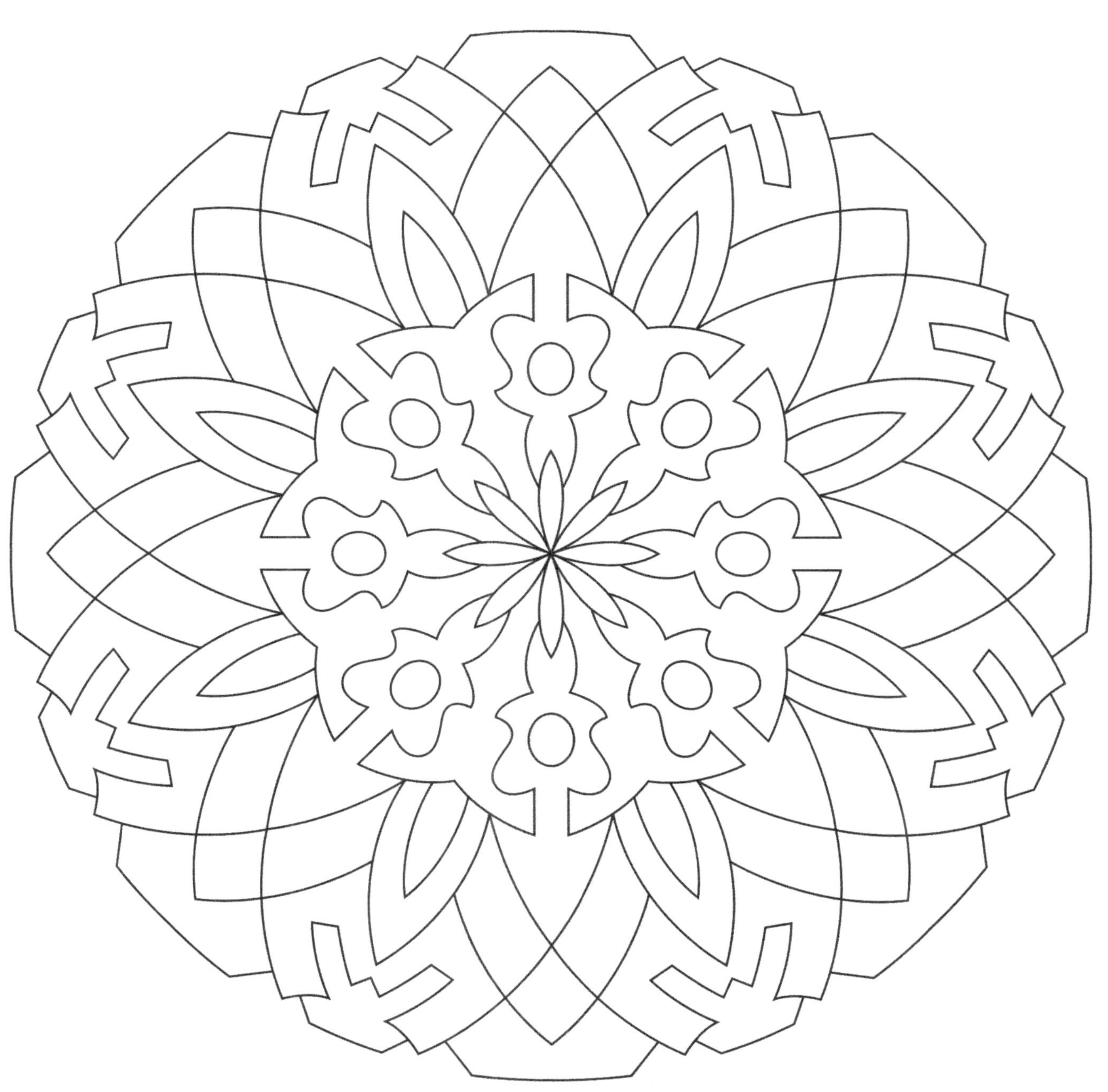

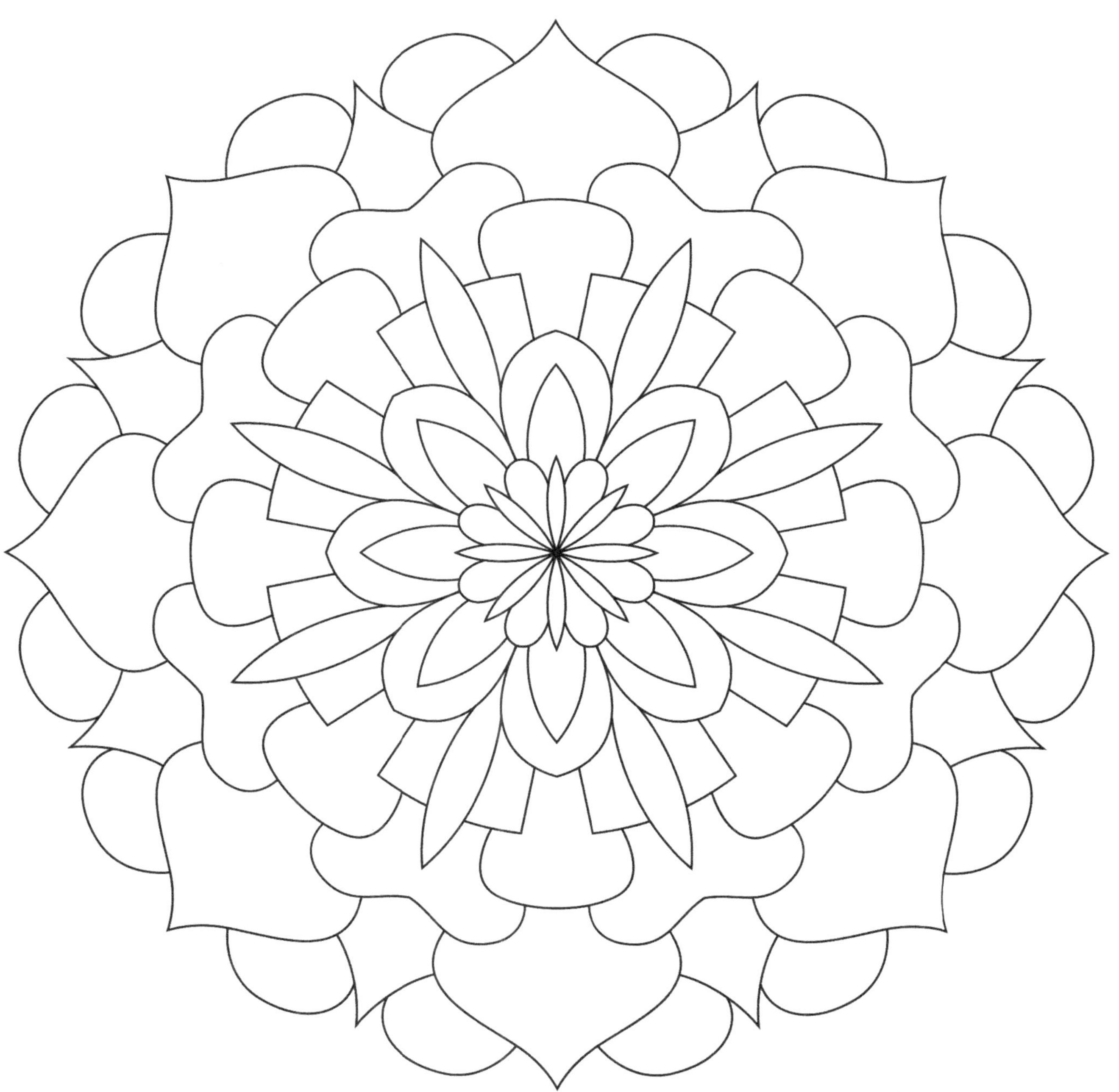

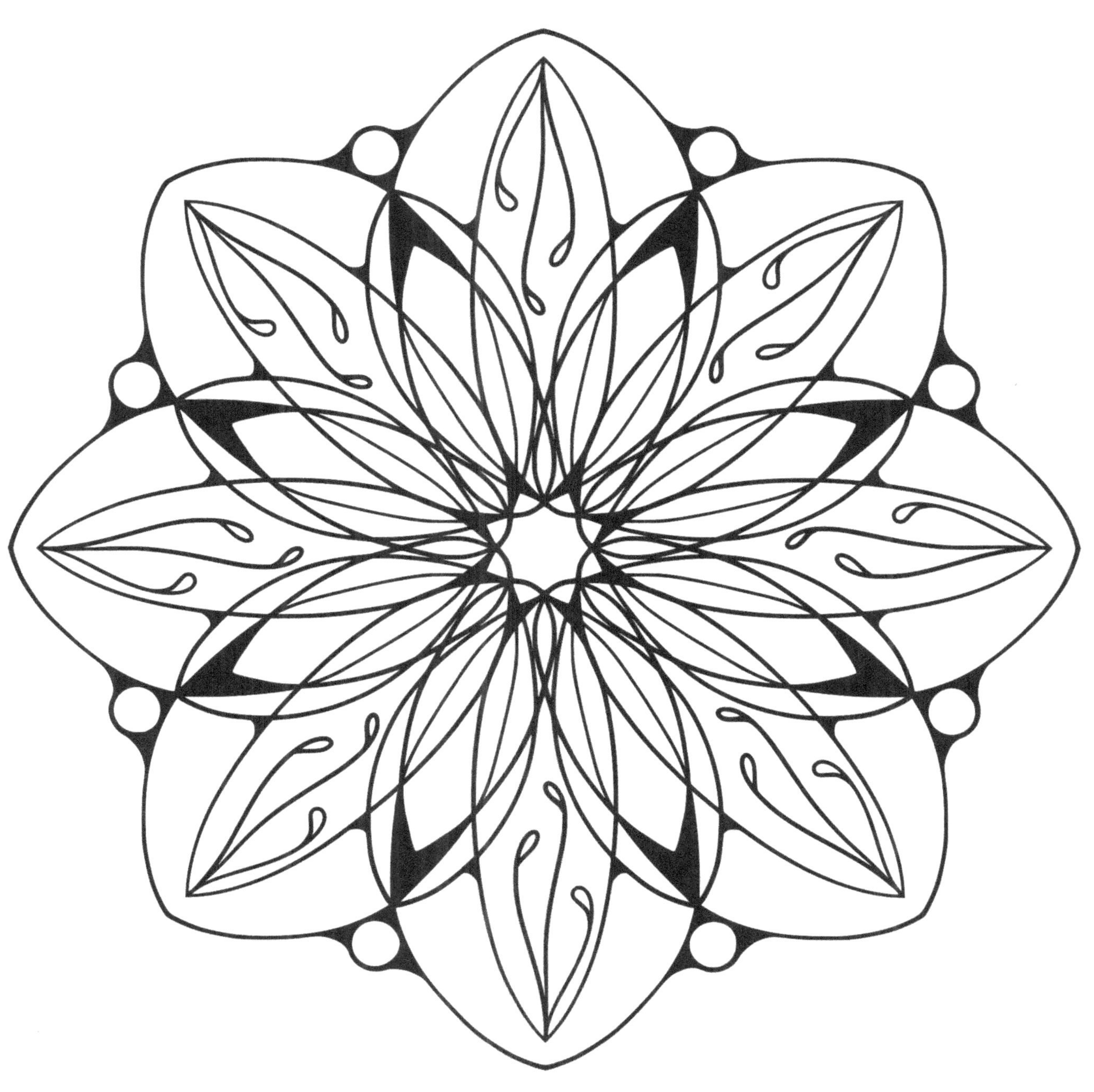

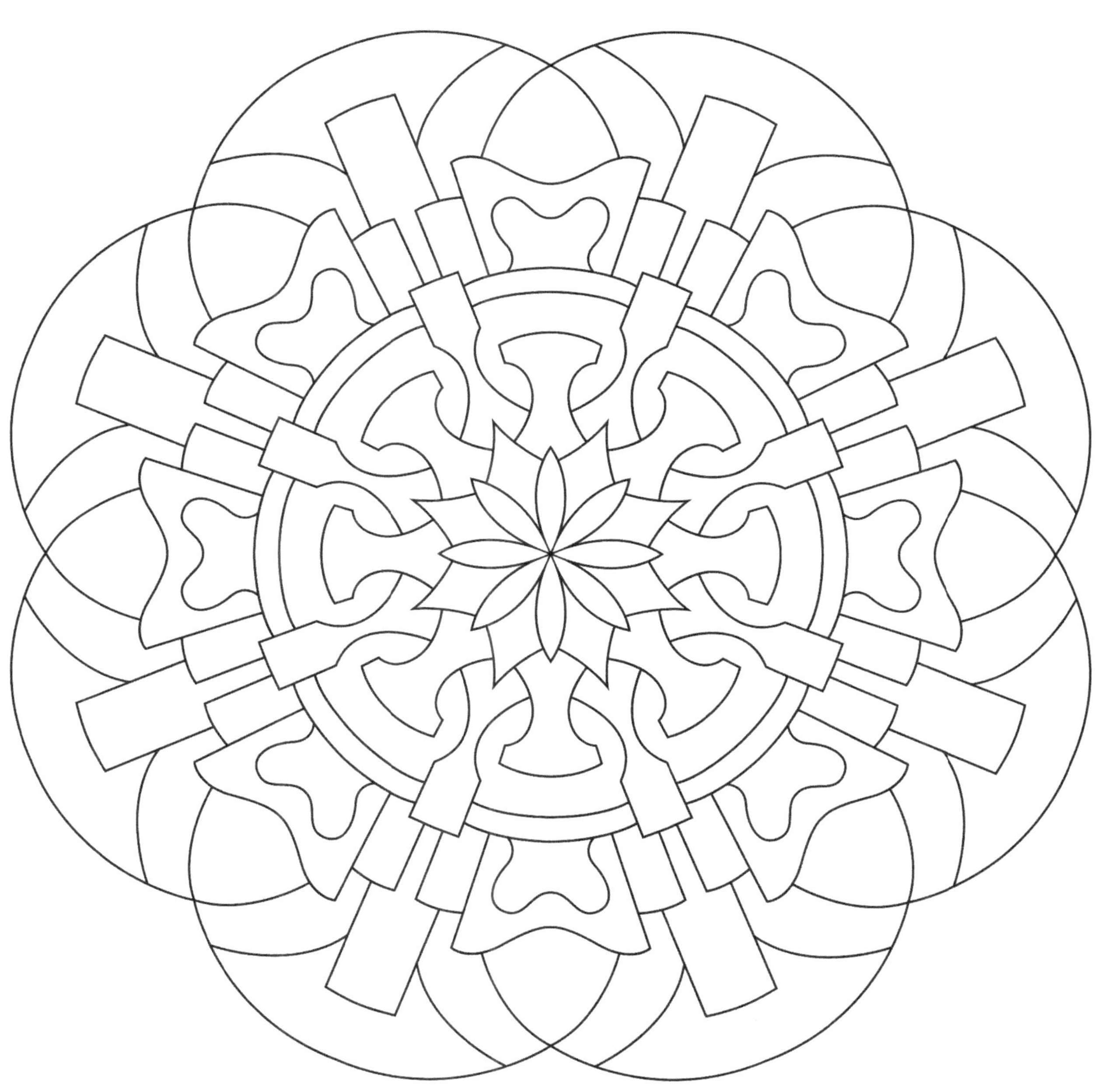

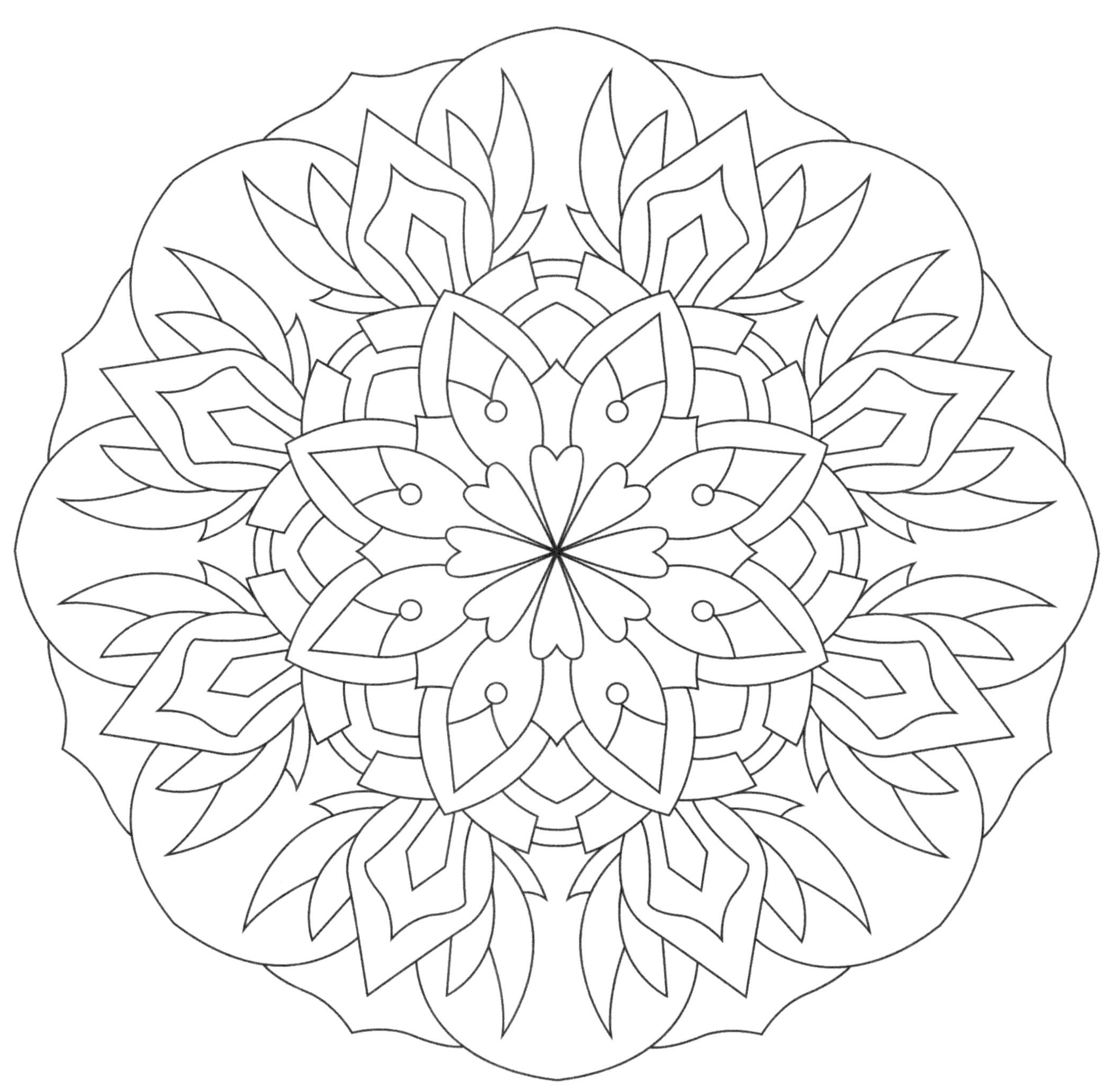

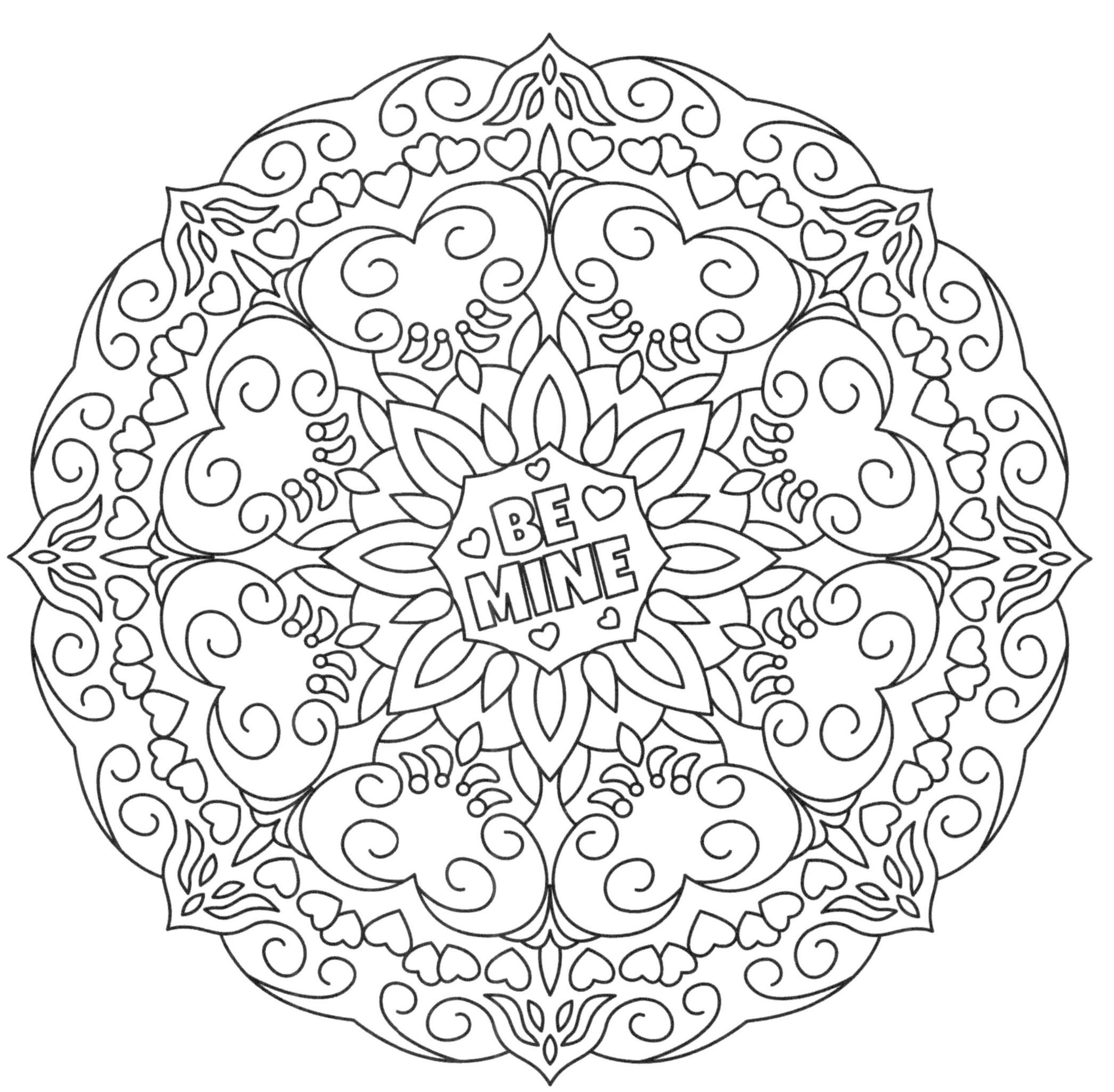
BE
MINE

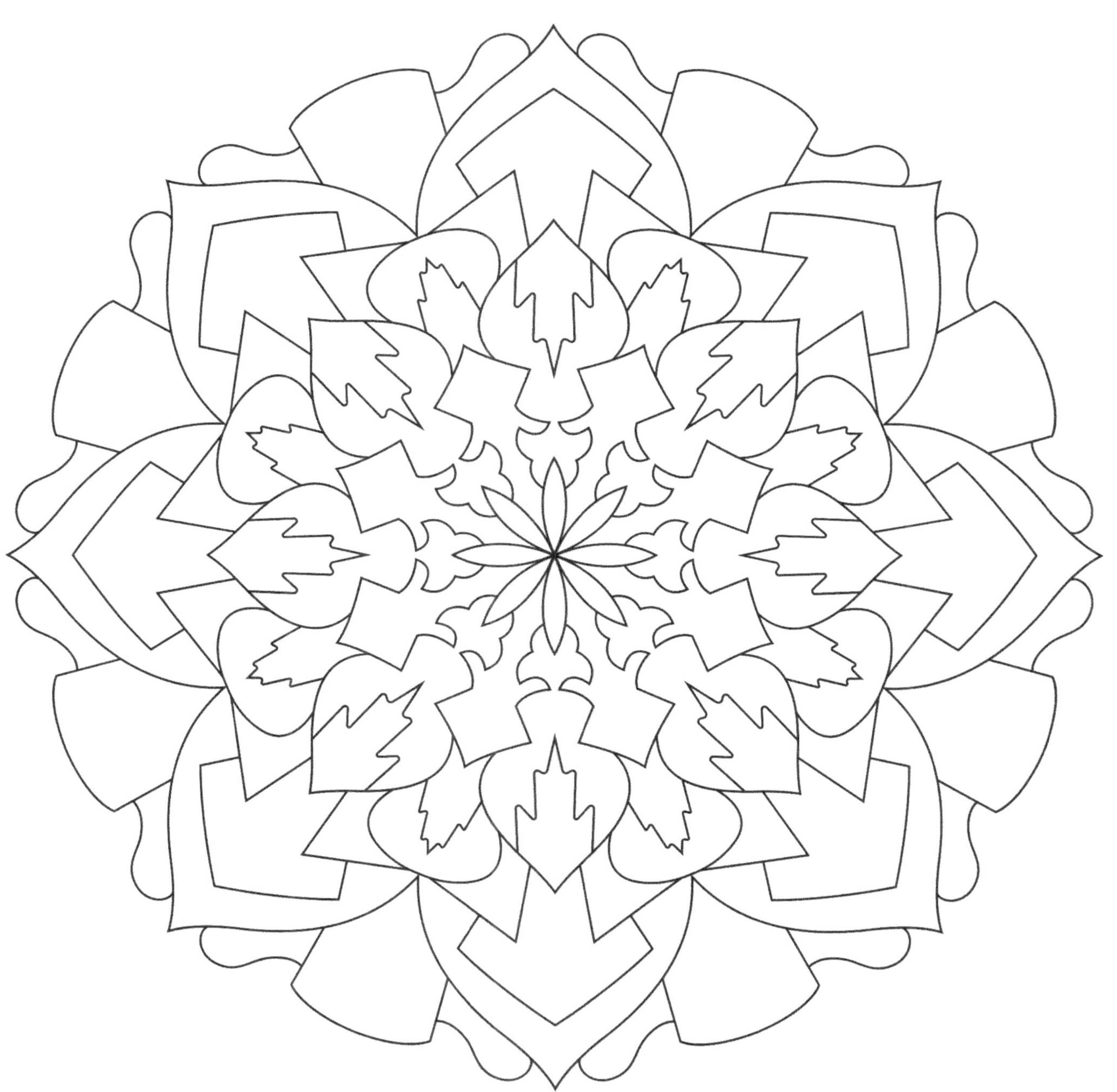

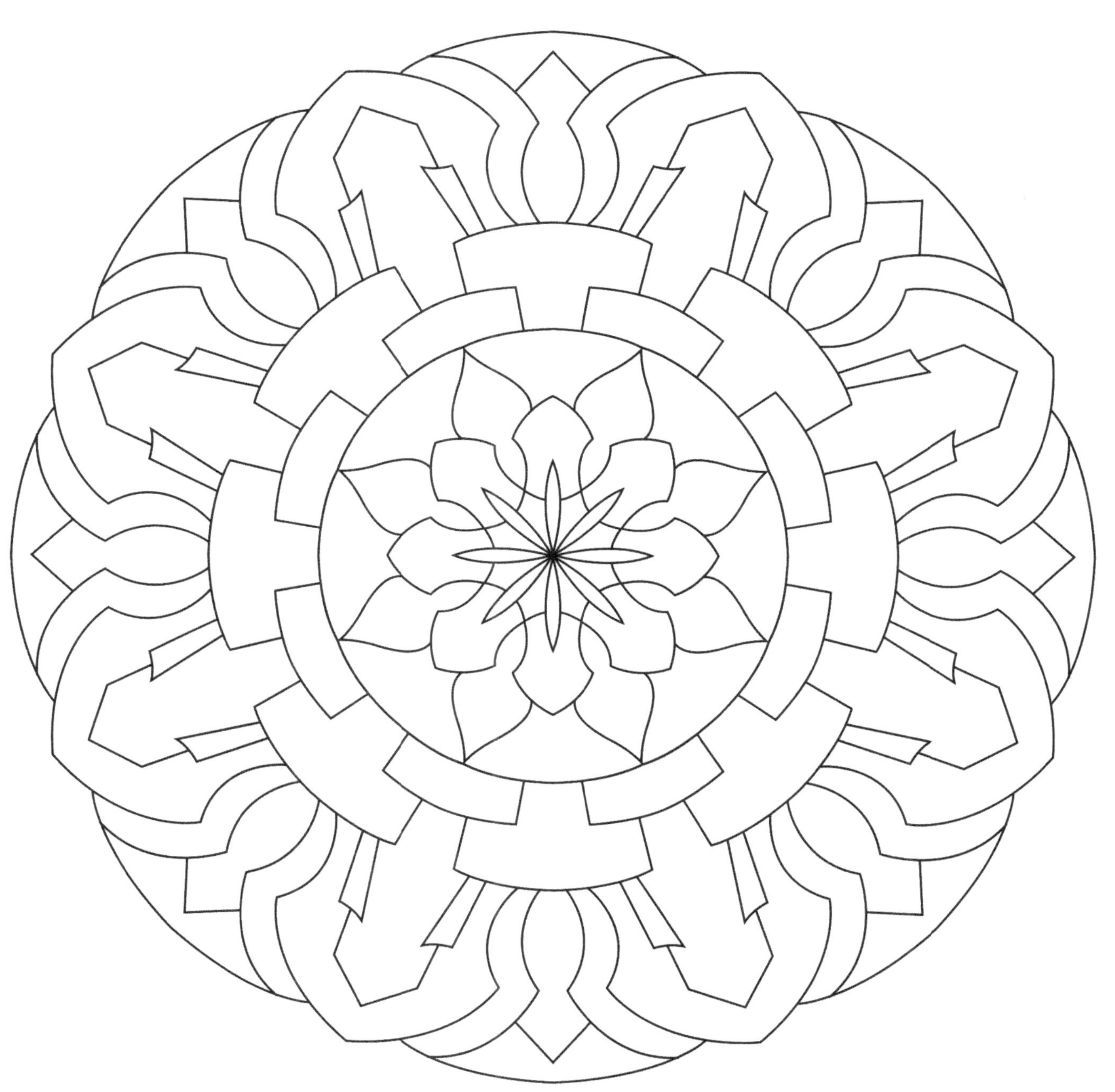

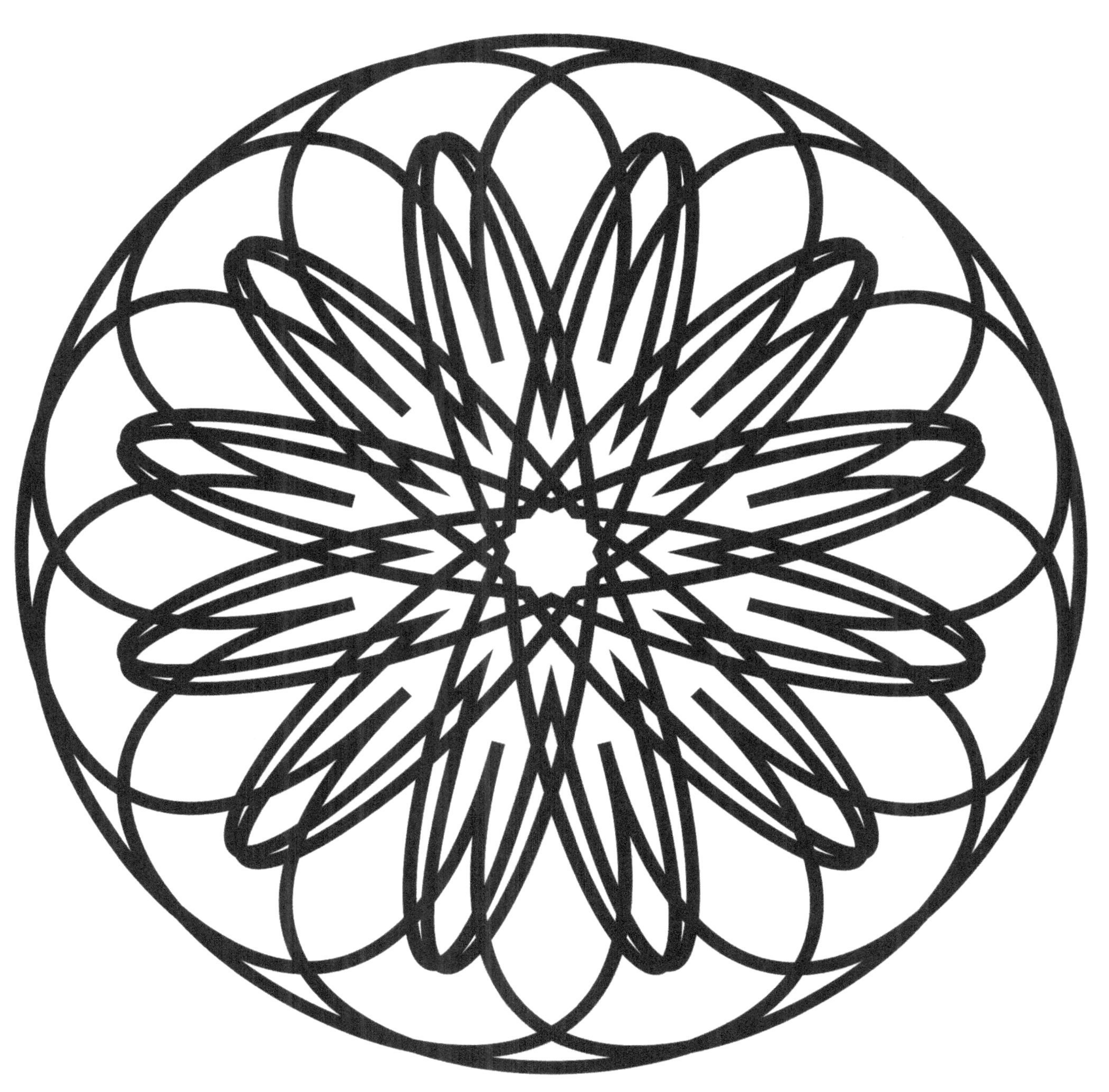

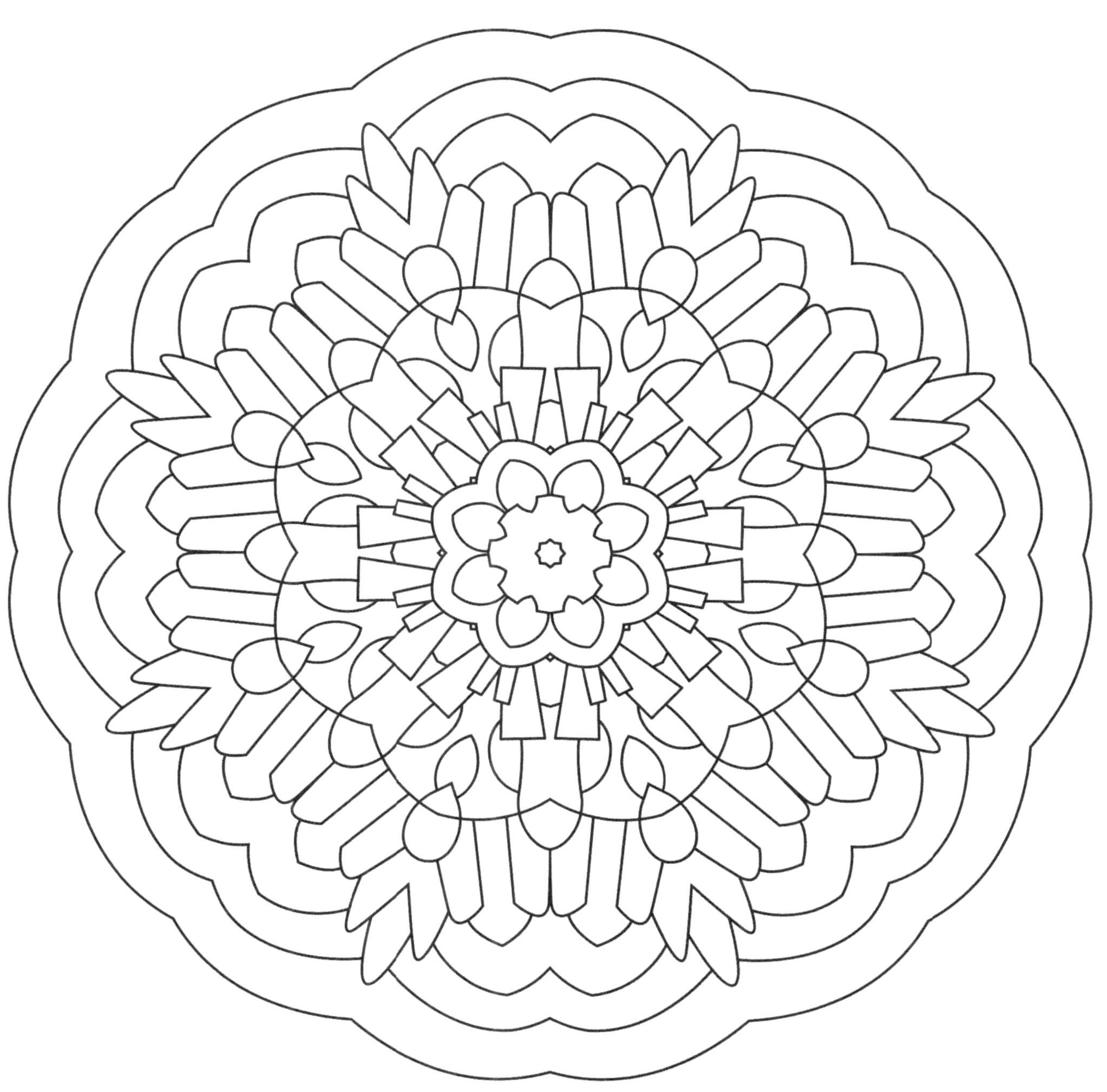

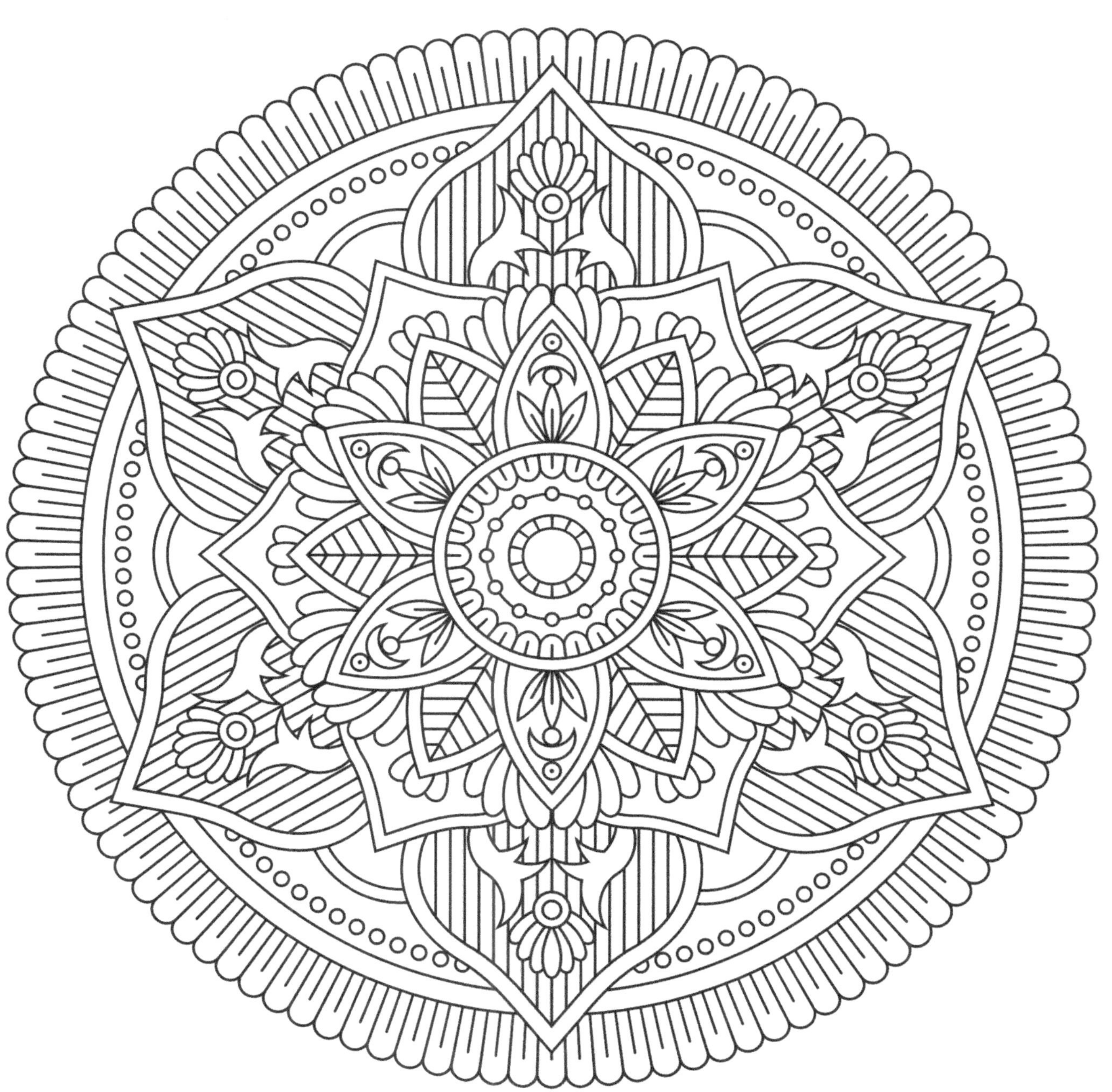

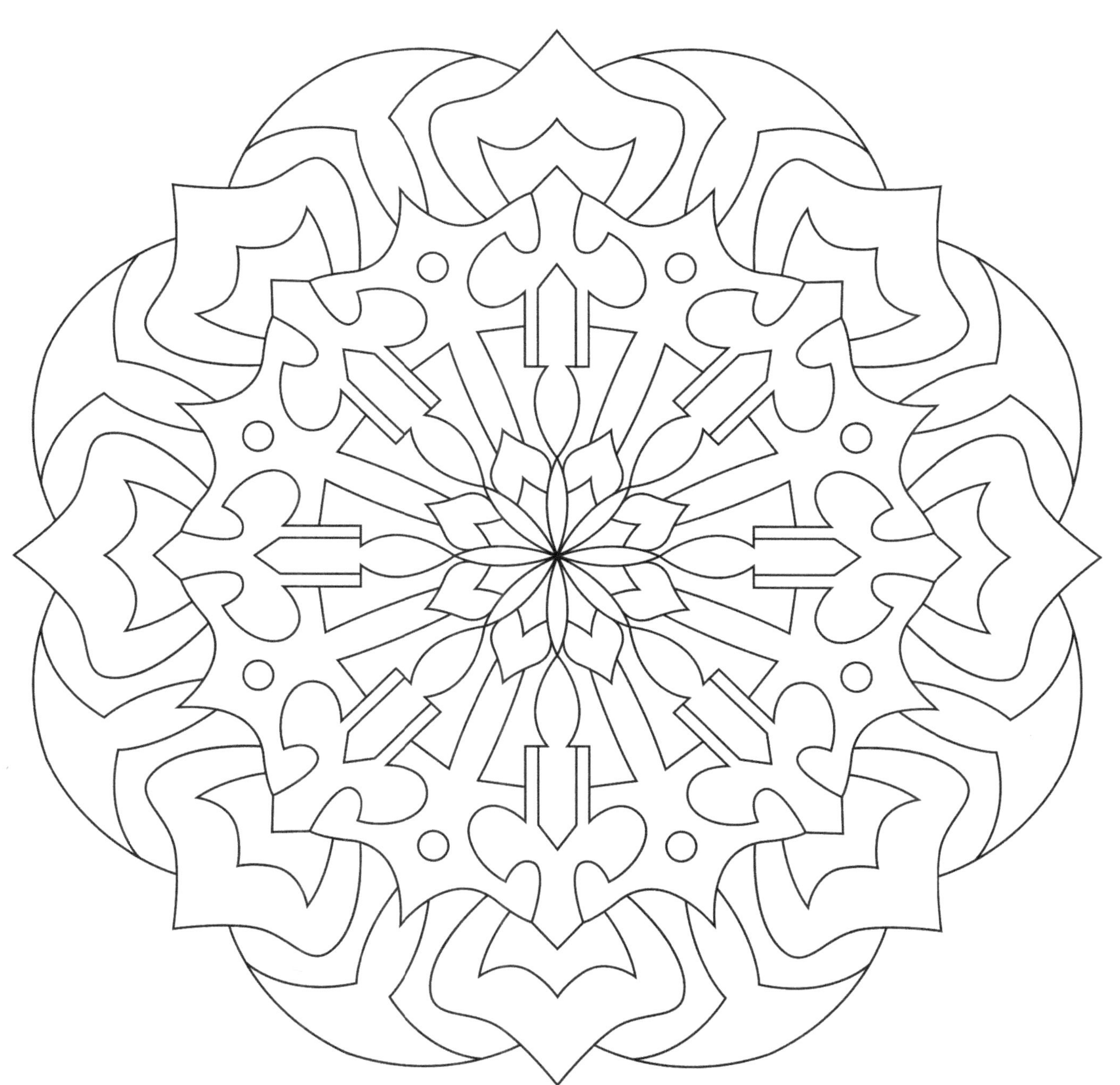

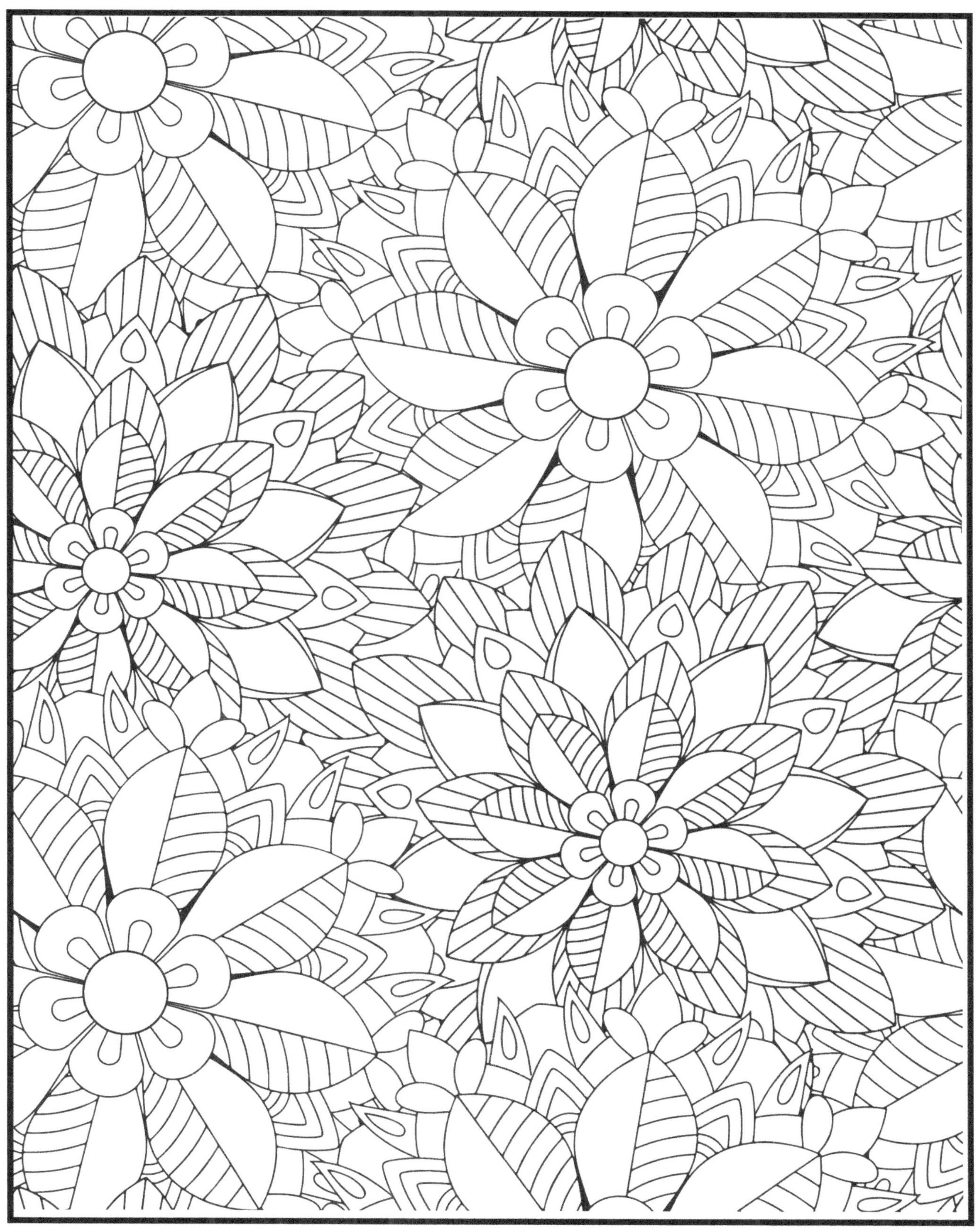

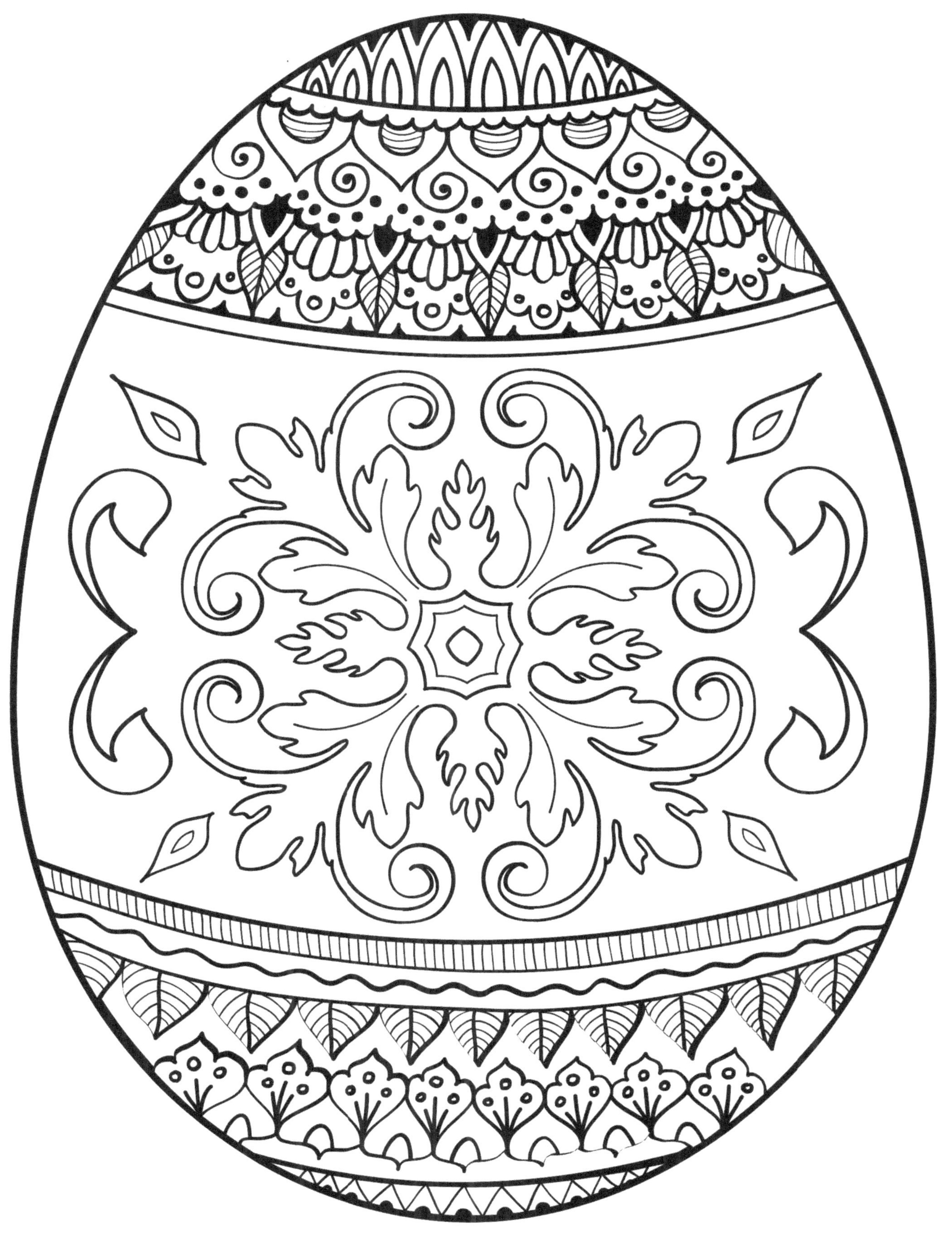

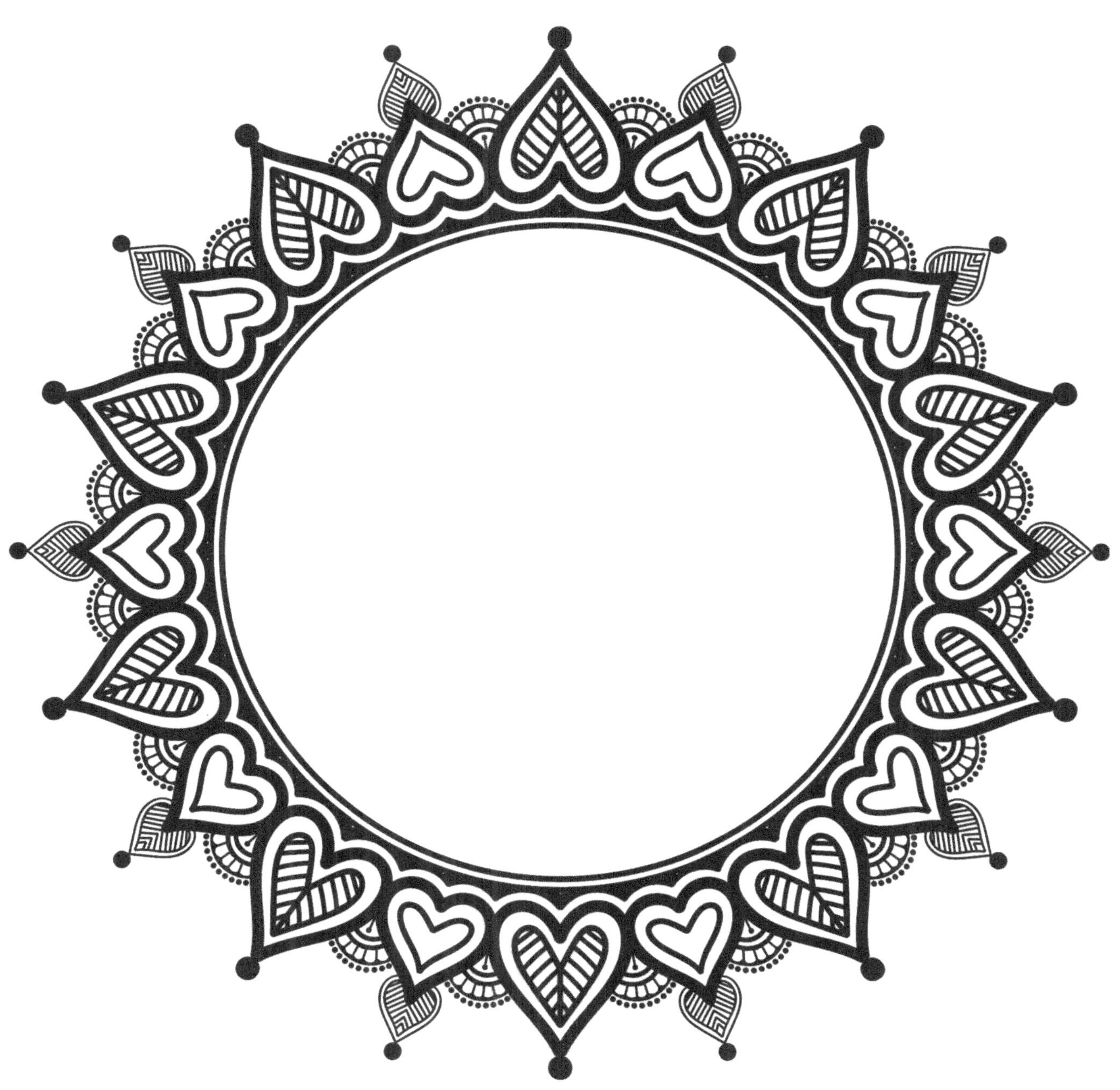

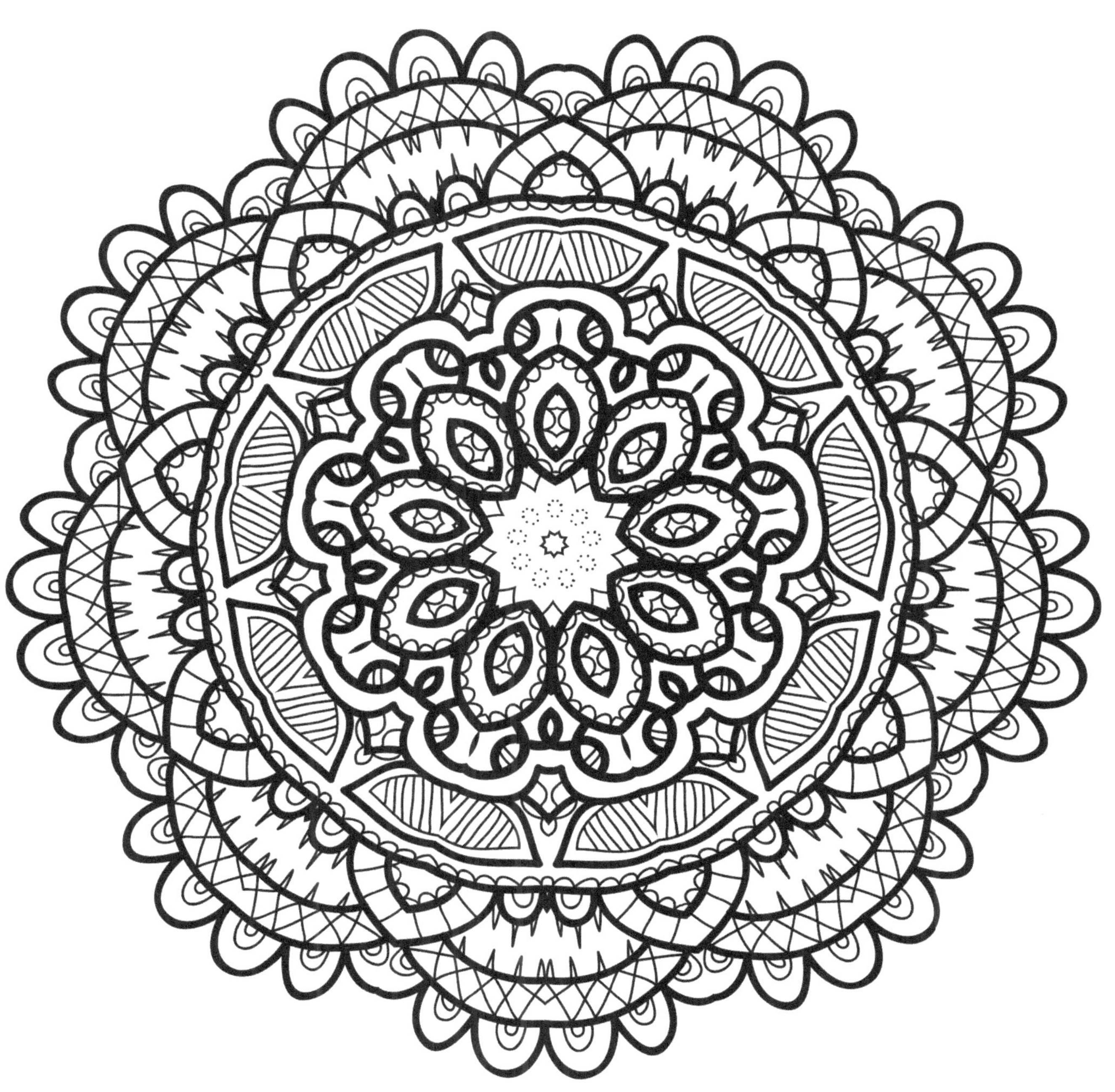

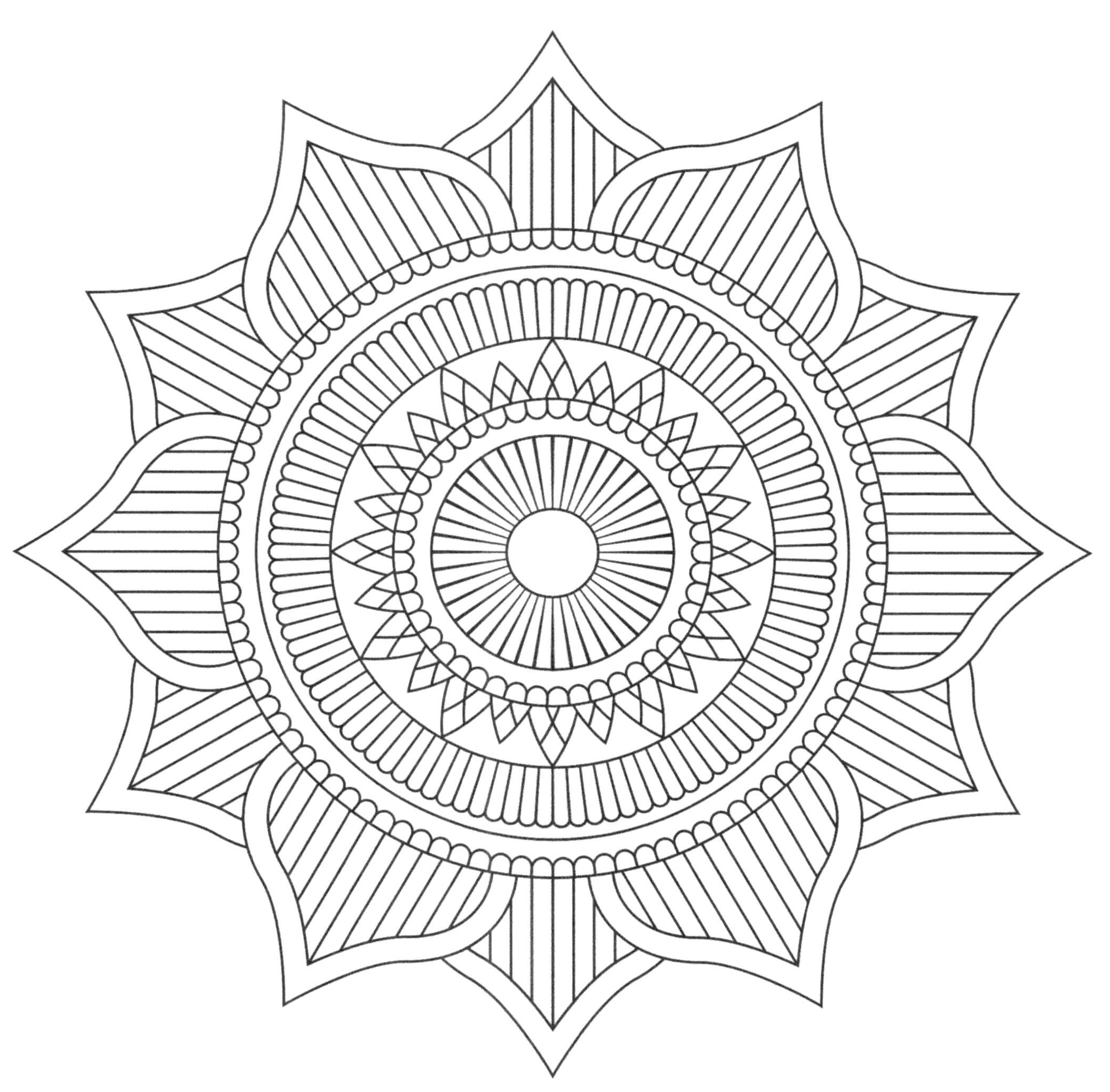

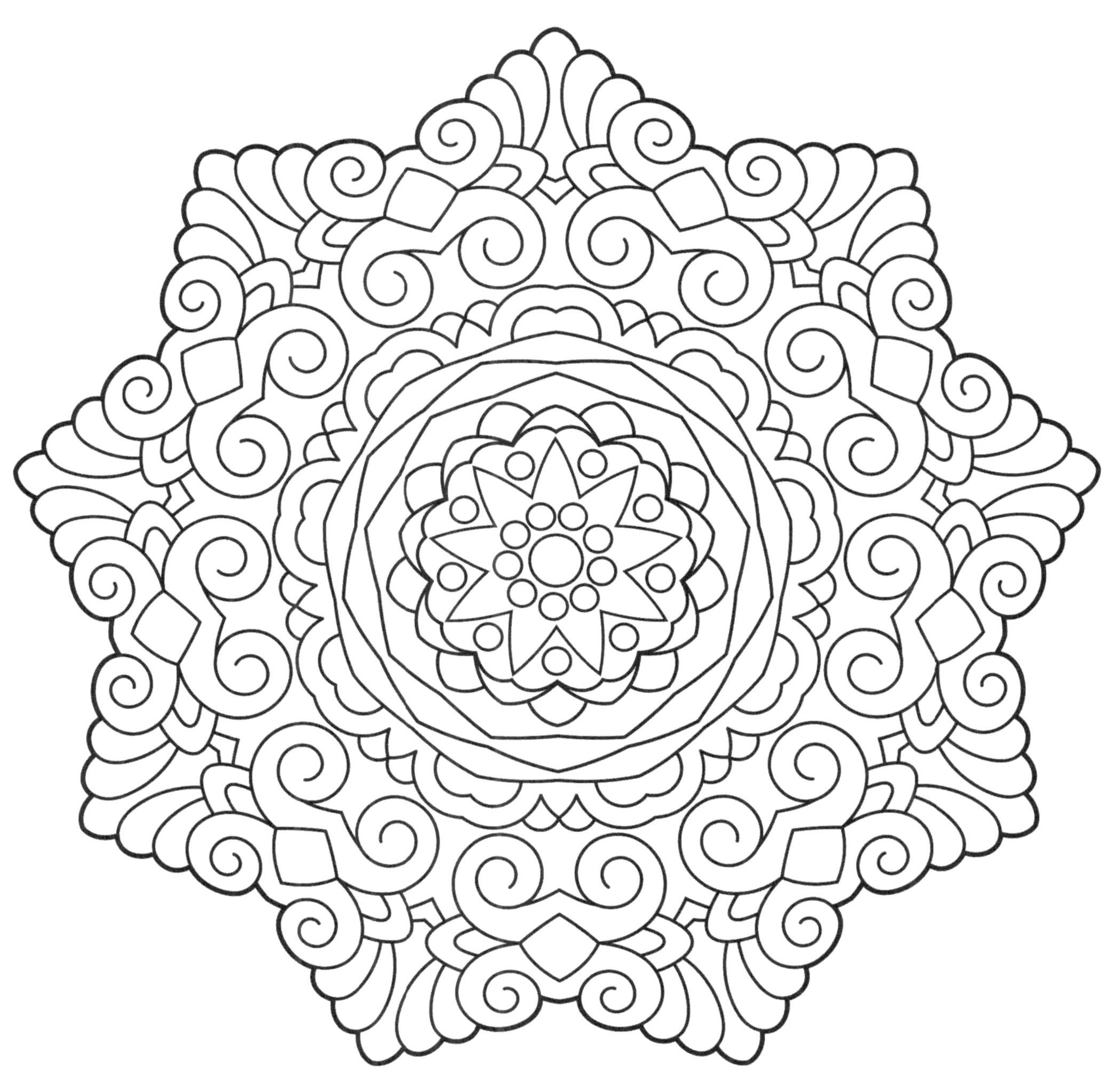

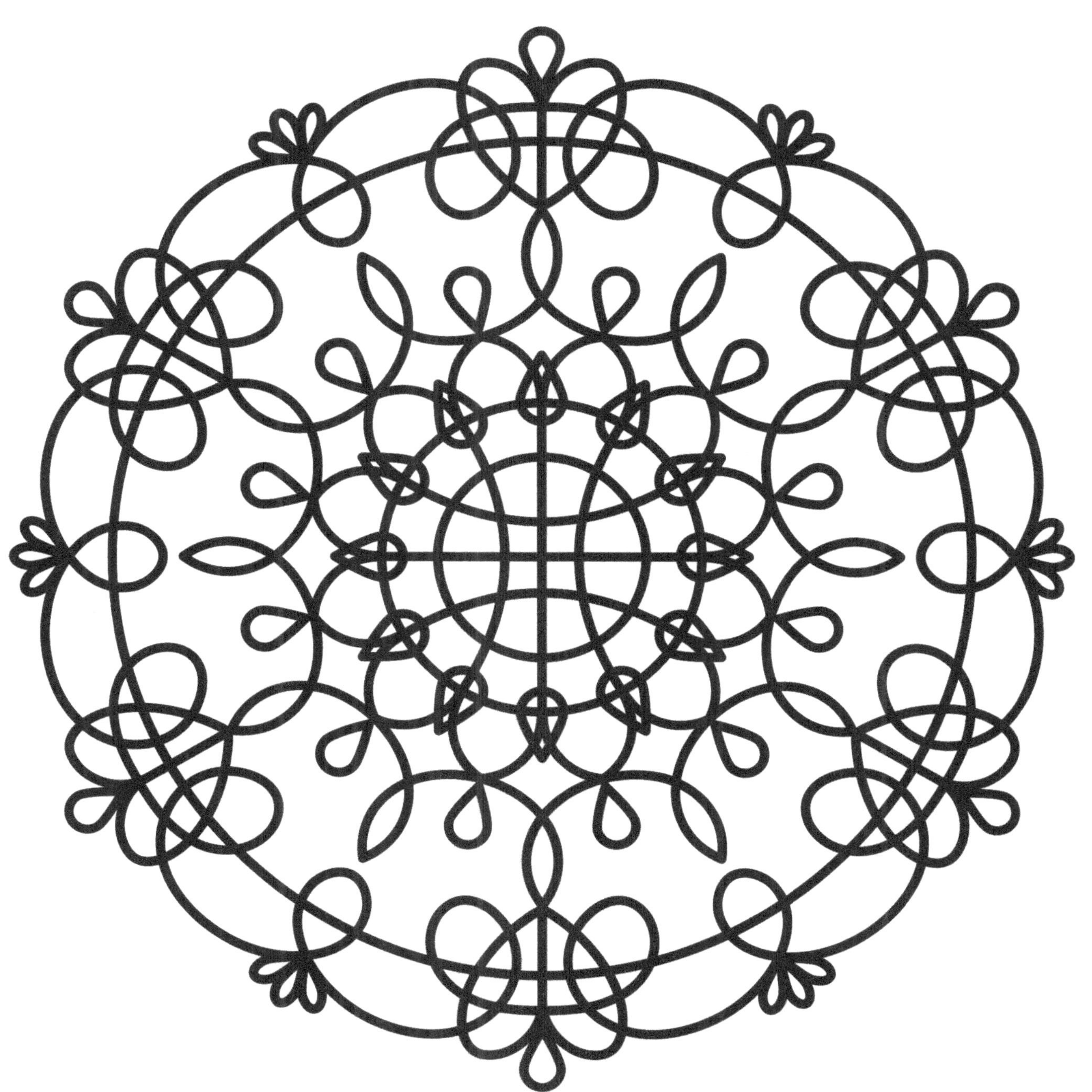

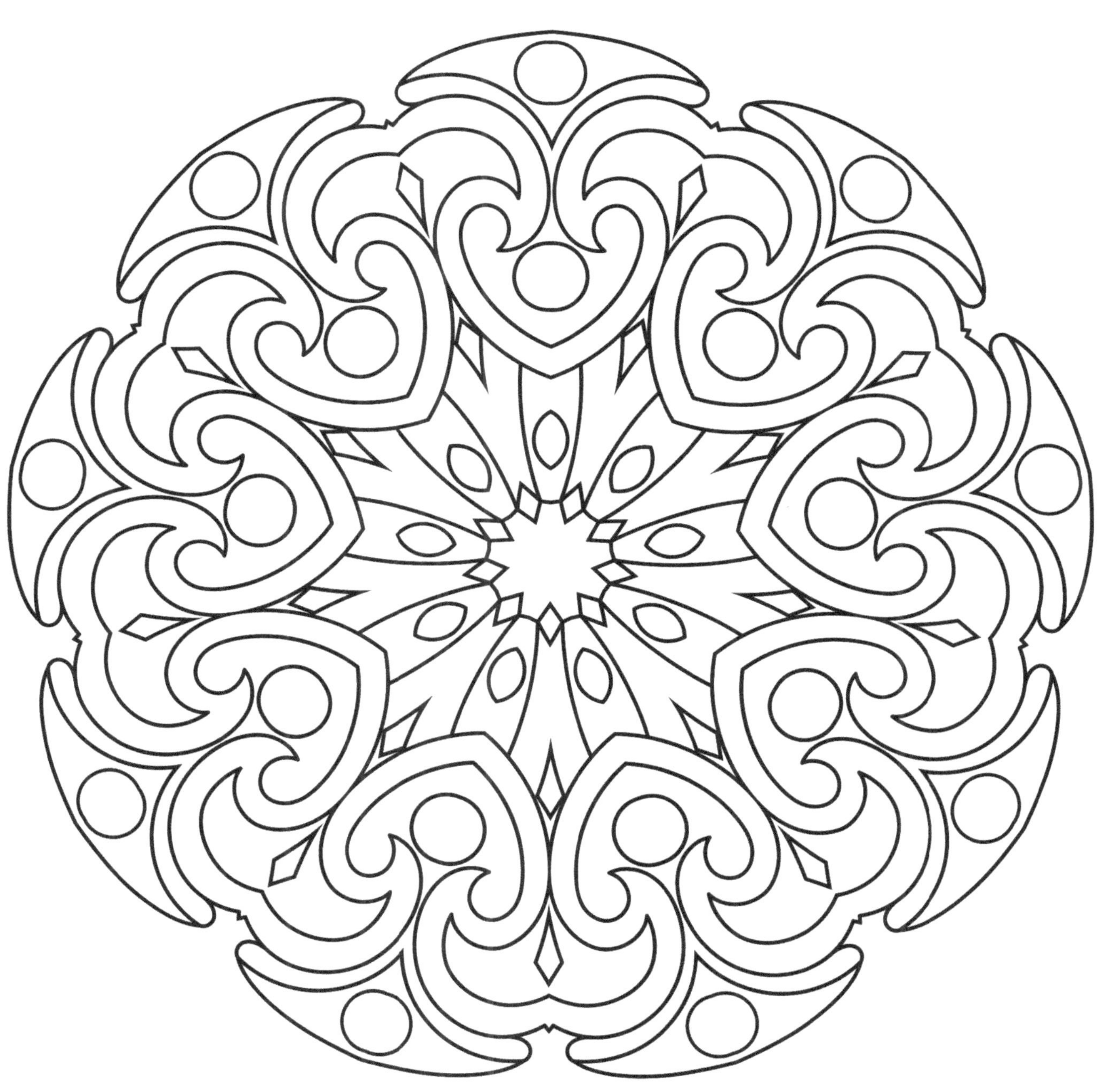